Wilderness Issues in the Arid Lands of the Western United States

Wilderness Issues in the Arid Lands of the Western United States

Edited by
Samuel I. Zeveloff and Cyrus M. McKell

University of New Mexico Press
Albuquerque

Library of Congress Cataloging-in-Publication Data

Wilderness issues in the arid lands of the western United States /
    edited by Samuel I. Zeveloff and Cyrus M. McKell.—1st ed.
        p.   cm.
    Includes bibliographical references and index.
    ISBN 0-8263-1365-5
    1. Nature conservation—Government policy—West (U.S.)   2. Arid
regions ecology—Government policy—West (U.S.)   3. Environmental
policy—West (U.S.)   4. Wilderness areas—Government policy—West
(U.S.)   5. Wildlife management—Government policy—West (U.S.)
I. Zeveloff, Samuel I., 1950–   .   II. McKell, C. M.
QH76.5.W34W55   1992
333.78′2′0978—dc20   92–4070
                                                                  CIP

DEDICATIONS

To my daughters: Abigail, Naomi, and Susannah
    with love,
          SIZ

To my wife: Betty
    with love,
          CMM

Contents

Tables

Figures

PREFACE

The purpose of this volume is to explore some of the cogent issues involved in designating and managing arid land wilderness. Arid lands are frequently suggested to be sparse, even desolate habitats without much to recommend them. Most often, we hear of them in such contexts as the wastelands of the Mojave Desert, the bombing range at White Sands, New Mexico, or the barren landscape of the Yucca Flats atomic test site in Nevada. It is only recently that the first U.S. national park was established in the vast Basin and Range geological province of the Southwest: Great Basin National Park in eastern Nevada. (Several other national parks occur in arid lands, primarily within the Colorado Plateau. However, they were created in large part because of their unusual geological features, not through efforts to preserve a diversity of arid habitats.) We emphasize that until recently, arid lands have been virtually excluded from wilderness consideration. Our introductory chapter explores the unique aspects of designating and managing wilderness in arid lands.

The chapter by Congressman Wayne Owens considers the political implications of such wilderness designation. As described, the outcome of these preservation efforts is determined by political processes, and the current atmosphere surrounding these activities is highly charged. Many in the ranching and mining industries, in particular, are opposed to more wilderness. It is thus important to include this political discussion, a version of which was published in the Southern Utah Wilderness Alliance newsletter (1989: vol. 6, No. 3). Congressman Owens is regarded by many as the chief legislative proponent of wilderness.

Foremost among the rationales for establishing natural areas is the desire to preserve biodiversity. Arid land wilderness ecosystems are no different in this regard. Yet these lands are ecologically unique and thus present special problems in the management of biotic resources. Three chapters address wildlife and aquatic resources management problems in arid lands. Some of the issues discussed in this section are not on designated wilderness per se. They are, however, associated with areas largely managed as nature preserves and thus exemplify some of the unique management problems facing such places in arid habitats. Carl Marti addresses management issues facing the Snake River Birds of Prey Area in southern Idaho. There are several competing resource interests in this area, some of which interfere with preservation of this important habitat for raptorial birds.

The chapter by Mark Boyce, Lee Metzgar, and Terry Peters addresses conflicts between feral horses and bighorn sheep in Montana's Bighorn Canyon

National Recreation Area. This is an interesting case study of management issues involving exotic and native species on federal lands. Its conclusions about regulating feral horses has implications for arid land wilderness throughout the West.

Fisheries and other aquatic resources may not be commonly considered as important concerns in arid habitats. Yet it is precisely because of the limited supply of water, and its uneven distribution patterns, that fisheries and related issues are so vital in these areas. This topic is reviewed by John and William Sigler, who have published extensively on arid land fishes.

The importance of successful wildlife management in natural areas cannot be overstated. In their treatise on the relationship between wildlife species and wilderness, Hendee and Schoenfeld (1978) explain how these entities are inextricably linked. They suggest that a clear wilderness philosophy is needed as a foundation for a sound wildlife management policy. Indeed, they echo the sentiments of many conservationists in suggesting that management of wilderness for wildlife will be a measure of our success in reaching an entente between economic development and environmental degradation.

The chapter by Cy McKell, Chris Call, and Allen Rasmussen presents the viewpoint of a group claiming to be impacted negatively by wilderness: the ranching industry. There are many misconceptions concerning the legality and disruptive nature of ranching activity in wilderness areas. Though permitted, ranching may only occur in a prescribed manner—and the resources upon which it depends may not be as accessible after wilderness designation. These authors review the perceived and real negative impacts of wilderness on ranching in arid lands.

In a sense, the chapter by Dick Carter of the Utah Wilderness Association is a rejoinder to the previous one. It presents compelling personal aesthetic justifications for preserving the uniquely beautiful natural history of southern Utah's wild areas.

The primary issue facing politicians in the wilderness designation process is the economic impact of such preservation. Indeed, the very concept of wilderness has been attacked as being far too costly (see, for example, Woolf 1990). This topic is first broached in the chapter by Wayne Owens, who considers the impact of arid-land wilderness designation on the economy of southern Utah. For a treatment of the economics of arid-land wilderness preservation and management, we have included the chapter by Richard Alston.

This book is not intended to provide an exhaustive treatment of every issue concerning arid land wilderness. Rather, we attempt to provide an in-depth look at some of the vital issues, particularly by presenting telling case studies of the problems that are being confronted now, and are likely to arise in the future. Our approach is deliberately interdisciplinary, seeking to cover arid-land wilderness issues from diverse perspectives.

The ethical justification for such preservation has previously been addressed, for example, in classic works such as Edward Abbey's *Desert Solitaire* by Edward Abbey (1968). Hopefully, areas not covered herein, such as the ecosystem management strategy (for example, see Agee and Johnson 1988, Grumbine 1990), will be covered in future volumes. Such an approach should be useful as designation and management decisions are made. Finally, we suggest that symposia on BLM arid land wilderness, similar to those organized by the Forest Service, be held and that their proceedings be published. These Forest Service volumes (Lucas 1986, 1987) have provided useful overviews of wilderness research and management issues.

This book is an outgrowth of a symposium held at the annual meeting of the American Association for the Advancement of Science in February 1990. Chapters include extended versions of presentations at the symposium as well as invited contributions. The illustrations in Chapter 5 ("Aquatic Resources of the Arid West: Perspectives on Fishes and Wilderness Management" by John W. Sigler and William F. Sigler) are by Sophie Sheppard from *Fishes of the Great Basin: A Natural History* by William F. Sigler and John F. Sigler (University of Nevada Press, 1987). They are reproduced by permission of the publisher. We acknowledge the assistance of Arthur Herschman and Elizabeth Zeutschel of AAAS in administering the symposium. Financial assistance for this conference and volume was provided by Weber State University.

REFERENCES

Abbey, E. 1968. *Desert Solitaire*. New York: Ballantine Books.

Agee, J. K., and D. R. Johnson (eds.) 1988. *Ecosystem Management for Parks and Wilderness*. Seattle: University of Washington Press.

Grumbine, R. E. 1990. "Viable Populations, Reserve Size, and Federal Lands Management: A Critique." *Conservation Biology* 4:127–134.

Hendee, J. C., and C. A. Schoenfeld. 1978. "Wilderness Management for Wildlife: Philosophy, Objectives, Guidelines." *Transactions of the 43d North American Wildlife and Natural Resources Conference* 43:331–343.

Lucas, R. C. (comp.) 1986. *Proceedings—National Wilderness Research Conference: Current Research*. United States Department of Agriculture Forest Service General Technical Report INT-212.

———. (comp.) 1987. *Proceedings—National Wilderness Research Conference: Issues, State-of-knowledge, Future Directions*. United States Department of Agriculture Forest Service General Technical Report INT-220.

Woolf, J. 1990. "Economist Says Wilderness Plan May Cost Utah Billions." *The Salt Lake Tribune*, 23 March: B1.

1

ARID LAND WILDERNESS ISSUES

Samuel I. Zeveloff and Cyrus M. McKell

INTRODUCTION

The United States is probably in its final phase of adding federally designated wilderness areas to its National Wilderness Preservation System. Though some lands may be added in the future, we are now in the last "major thrust" of doing so. Coincidentally, this activity is occurring on the heels of the twenty-fifth anniversary of the Wilderness Act of 1964.

Protection of natural areas in the U.S. began at least as far back as 1872 with the creation of our first national park, Yellowstone. The setting aside of wilderness, those areas which are to remain free from development, did not begin until some fifty years later. In 1924, the eminent ecologist Aldo Leopold spearheaded the establishment of our first wilderness: 574,000 acres of New Mexico's Gila National Forest (see, for example, Flader 1978, Johnson 1989). Others instrumental in developing rationales for wilderness preservation include David Brower, Arthur Carhart, Robert Marshall, and Howard Zahniser (see, for example, Baldwin 1967, Mealey 1988). Their efforts culminated in the signing of the Wilderness Act. Through this act, a National Wilderness Preservation System, originally consisting of over nine million acres, was established.

Arguments for wilderness are usually centered on the necessity of maintaining parts of Earth in a natural, "pristine" state (see, for example, Bainbridge 1984). This is becoming an ever more urgent task, as the destruction of habitats and species is proceeding at a frighteningly accelerated pace. In fact, the protection of many species, particularly large, wide-ranging ones, is only possible within the confines of sizable natural areas. The importance of preserving biodiversity, the richness of our planet's life, has been effectively argued for economical as well as ethical reasons (see, for example, Ledec and Goodland 1988, Wilson 1988).

Most of the current proposed additions to the wilderness system are lands that previously would not have been considered for wilderness designation. These are the arid lands of North America's Great Basin and Southwest: deserts, the canyons of the Colorado Plateau and similar formations, and a variety of other arid landscapes. Indeed, our very thinking about what constitutes wilderness has undergone an evolution. The wilderness areas envisaged from the early part of this century through the present typically were majestic, high mountain regions. Only within the last few years has there been a concerted effort to designate arid lands as wilderness areas.

By anyone's definition, the term *arid land* is hard to pin down. These lands are normally defined as areas with deficient precipitation (see, for example, McGinnies 1988), or those in which actual evapotranspiration exceeds precipitation (Goudie and Wilkinson 1977, Evenari 1981, Crawford and Gosz 1986). Others suggest that a high variation in the factors regulating ecosystem stability, such as temperature and precipitation, best characterizes arid habitats (see, for example, MacMahon 1981). In any case, these lands are usually marginal in biological productivity (Battisse 1988). A lack of precipitation necessary for traditional agricultural practices occurs in some 43% of the earth's lands (McGinnies 1988). Arid land habitats are diverse and include "true" deserts, dry steppes, and prairies. There is no overall pattern of correlations between climate and vegetation that is useful in establishing a classification scheme for arid lands (McGinnies 1988).

Due to their ecological vulnerability, their tremendous land mass, their importance to adjacent land uses, and their low utility for food production, arid lands have been the subject of intensive investigation (see, for example, Whitehead et al. 1988). In 1947, UNESCO suggested the establishment of international arid zone laboratories, an idea that became a reality in 1951. The goal of these stations was to better understand arid land ecosystems and ultimately to help nations develop their resources (Batisse 1988). Many arid and semiarid land ecosystems have undergone extreme disturbances, such as desertification, due to overgrazing and other poor resource management practices (see, for example, papers in Allen 1988).

Efforts such as the Man and the Biosphere program, beginning in 1968, enhanced understanding and the attempt to reconcile differences between those concerned with environmental conservation versus development. These programs were also useful in addressing arid-land conservation problems. The United States is in an enviable position, however, in being able to consider reserving large portions of its arid lands for preservation without having to concentrate solely on resource development. We are not alone in this regard. The importance of establishing arid land preserves has also been articulated for Mexico's Chihuahuan and Sonoran deserts (Aguirre and Maury 1988, González-Romero et al. 1988, respectively), for the Atacama in Chile (Torres and Rodríguez 1988), and others (see Whitehead et al. 1988). Nevertheless, most nations simply do not have the luxury of establishing preservation zones in arid lands, which are far too much in demand for their mineral and forest products or for direct food production and grazing.

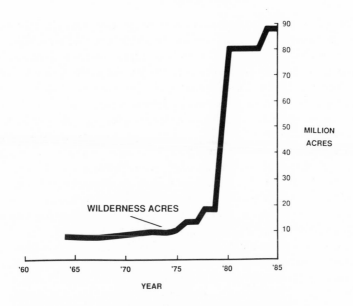

Figure 1.1. Trends in the size of the National Wilderness Preservation System from 1964 to 1985 (modified from Lucas 1987).

THE LANDS AT STAKE

Approximately 91.5 million acres (about 37 million hectares or 143,000 square miles) are in the National Wilderness Preservation System. In all, there are 474 separate areas, which are highly variable in size. They cover a land mass about the size of Montana, or 4% of the United States. Just over 60% of the total acreage is in Alaska, primarily as a result of wilderness legislated by the Alaska National Interest Lands and Conservation Act of 1980. Area added by this act virtually tripled the amount of designated wilderness at that time (Figure 1.1).

The four agencies that manage wilderness in the United States are the Forest Service (FS), National Park Service (NPS), Fish and Wildlife Service (FWS), and Bureau of Land Management (BLM). The first is a unit of the U.S. Department of Agriculture; the latter three are under the U.S. Department of Interior. When the Wilderness Act was passed in 1964, it essentially ignored lands administered by the BLM. It is likely that the preeminent activities on these lands, such as ranching and mining, made it politically difficult to consider them as wilderness. Furthermore, the typically low productivity and aridity of BLM areas made them seem less desirable as wilderness than the alpine regions of the other agencies.

The BLM has had a controversial history since its inception in 1946, result-ing from the consolidation of the Grazing Service and the General Land Office (see Muhn and Stuart 1988). BLM lands are often regarded as the relatively unproductive public domain that remained after the more "desirable" places were set aside: as parks and monuments of the National Park Service, the valuable timber-producing units of the Forest Service, and the significant wildlife habitats of the Fish and Wildlife Service. Thus, BLM areas have been characterized as "leftover lands" (see, for example, Watkins 1989). Many of this agency's lands historically have been and currently are managed primar-ily for sheep and cattle grazing. Intensive uses such as mining also occur on these areas. It has often been suggested that the agency caters to the needs of these industries, to the detriment of wildlife habitat and scenic values.

In total, the BLM administers approximately 310 million acres. Excluding Alaska, there are some 175 million acres under its jurisdiction. This is a siz-able piece of real estate; almost equal to the combined total of 179 million acres administered in the lower forty-eight states by all of the other agencies (FS, NPS, FWS). Virtually all BLM lands are in eleven western states. How-ever, some relatively small holdings exist in Louisiana, Florida, and Wisconsin.

Due to the amount of land at stake, the shift in perspective concerning what constitutes wilderness, and consequent pressure from wilderness ad-vocates, Congress passed the Federal Land Policy and Management Act (FLPMA) in 1976. This act put an end to large-scale disposition of public lands, mandating that most of them were to remain under federal owner-ship. It also required both the BLM and Forest Service to determine how to best manage public lands for multiple uses. Of special significance to our dis-cussion is Section 603 of FLPMA. This directed the BLM to complete a wil-derness inventory and study of all of its lands (except those in Alaska) by 1991, and make a recommendation about which lands should receive such designa-tion. FLPMA has generated a considerable amount of controversy, mostly because it placed environmental and recreational interests in a position of legal equality with the historically dominant industries such as grazing and mining (Gregg 1988).

Currently, about twenty-five million acres involving 860 separate BLM areas are under consideration for wilderness designations (Figure 1.2). Many wil-derness advocates believe that this amount is too small, and that the BLM has omitted critical areas from consideration (Watkins 1989). Some have even charged that the agency has not protected the wilderness nature of the areas under review, which would be a legal violation of the review process (Ashen-felter 1990). To date, only some 467,000 acres of the land under review, involv-ing twenty-five areas, have been designated as wilderness. Over half of these are in Arizona, included as part of the Arizona Wilderness Act of 1984. Nevada has also recently passed a wilderness bill. With lands categorized as wilder-ness prior to FLPMA, BLM wilderness areas now include about 500,000 acres.

BLM WILDERNESS STUDY AREAS

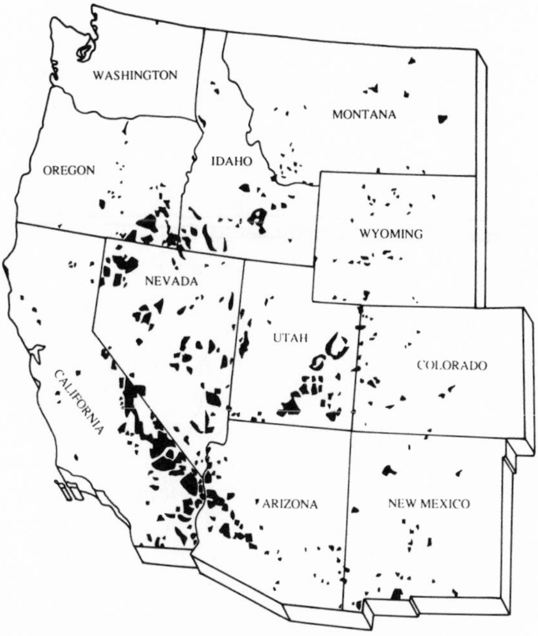

Figure 1.2. Bureau of Land Management areas under consideration
for wilderness designation (modified from *U.S. News and World
Report* 1989).

The process of determining which lands receive wilderness designation is
a considerably more circuitous matter involving more than just the BLM final-
izing a recommendation. The U.S. congressmen from each affected state then
must introduce their own proposals to Congress on this issue. The discussion
and voting ensuing from these proposals will determine which lands are to
be preserved. Currently, proposals have also been submitted by representatives from Utah and California, in addition to those from the states mentioned above.

A submitted wilderness proposal need not be agreed upon by a state's entire
congressional delegation. In Utah, there are presently two competing proposals: one introduced by Congressman Wayne Owens (D), the other by Congressman James Hansen (R). Clouding the picture further is the fact that some
groups, such as the Utah Wilderness Association, have their own proposals
(Thayn 1988). These are not submitted to Congress, but are intended to influence the decision-making process. Over the next several years, some major

battles are projected concerning the classification of BLM lands. Significantly, most of these lands are in arid environments.

FUTURE CONCERNS

It is certain that a sizable portion of the BLM lands under consideration as wilderness will be so designated. Even many of those opposed to proposals advocating the largest amounts for wilderness concede that some lands will be thus set aside. Congressman James Hansen of Utah, seen as hardly a strong wilderness advocate, has submitted a bill to designate 1.4 million acres of Utah as wilderness. Whatever the outcome of these various bills, many arid BLM areas will remain in their current status. Additional arid lands are under the jurisdiction of other federal and state agencies. All of these arid lands, not just those ultimately designated as wilderness, are in need of comprehensive and integrated management strategies.

Managing arid land wilderness presents some unique challenges. But before discussing these, we need to address how the very notion of managing wilderness seems to be a contradiction in terms. After all, a key aim in establishing these areas is to minimize human influence. Management, alternately, implies directing efforts toward achieving desired goals within limits of acceptable change (Stankey et al. 1985). The primary challenge, therefore, in wilderness management is to somehow ensure that these areas primarily remain affected only by natural forces (Fege 1990).

The initial acts of planning for and establishing wilderness areas involve management. Other management concerns include administering the utilization of range forage, minerals, and wildlife, inasmuch as their "harvesting" is permitted by law in wilderness areas. Further, the impacts of activities such as pollution (see, for example, Schreiber and Newman 1987), artillery shelling, and motorized vehicles in adjacent areas must be monitored to minimize effects on wilderness. An understanding of the natural ecological processes (for instance, succession) of wilderness ecosystems is critical to their management (see, for example, Franklin 1978). Similarly, Johnson and Agee (1988) discuss how viewing wildernesses as dynamic and flexible ecosystems is crucial to such administration. In all cases, the most successful wilderness management will be that in which its signs are minimized (Fege 1990).

Most proposed BLM arid-land wilderness areas are considerably "drier and flatter" than the "classic" Forest Service alpine wilderness areas (Burford 1987). Their major management problems have been reviewed by Burford (1987) and Porter (1987), and are as follows: arid lands are typically fragile; impacts by users tend to be slow to recover. Hence, the scheduling and rehabilitation of campsites, which are problems in any heavily utilized wilderness, will need even more attention in arid lands. Further, many proposed BLM wilderness areas are small compared to the established Forest Service areas. Moreover, in many cases they are but small fragments of ecosystems and thus are more likely to face outside pressures.

Many of the arid-land wilderness areas under review are located in "canyon country." Indeed, the extensive and often dramatic rock formations of canyons provide overwhelming aesthetic appeal. Unfortunately, canyons tend to funnel visitors and thus concentrate them. Already, this has proven to be a problem in Arizona's Aravaipa and Paria Canyon wilderness areas (Burford 1987, Porter 1987). Finally, the management of wildfires and their impact on wildlife management are of particular concern in arid lands (Porter 1987). The current fire policy in wilderness areas, to "let it burn" unless human life or property is threatened or another emergency situation arises, has been challenged (see, for example, Bonnicksen 1990).

A growing concern is the increase in military activities on BLM and other arid lands. These seem certain to impact wilderness areas. The U.S. Navy has arranged for a provision in the recently enacted Nevada Wilderness Act to permit unlimited low-level flights in four new wilderness areas. In Idaho, the Air Force plans to enlarge the Saylor Creek Bombing Range from 150,000 to 1.5 million acres of BLM land. This would position the range next to the Snake River Birds of Prey Area (see the chapter here by C. D. Marti). Low-level flights and live bombs are a particular problem for nesting birds. When military activities require the withdrawal of public lands, other uses are precluded. The public may wish to become involved in determining whether such changes are desirable (Mattox 1990), especially in view of proposed reductions in military spending following political changes in eastern European countries and Russia.

Ever since its settlement, the American West has been a battleground for water and the rights to it (see, for example, Meyer 1989). Upcoming legislative hearings on arid land wilderness will certainly have these issues brought to the fore. In such areas, the concerns over water are many. First, water sources are often ephemeral and seasonal. Stream channels, as well, are typically shallow. Therefore, these water sources generally can sustain little impact. Importantly, the wildlife in these areas are usually highly dependent on such limited water supplies (Starkey and Larson 1987). In addition, such areas often harbor significant archeological sites, for earlier native cultures were also dependent on them.

In alpine wilderness areas, water resources are comparatively well protected and pure because the headwaters of river and lakes are often located there and feed the remainder of the watershed. In arid lands, however, water is more likely to be intercepted en route, resulting in a lower quality level by the time it reaches a wilderness. Any attempts to secure more water, to require heightened flow, or to impose purity standards have been and are certain to continue to be opposed by competing users of this limited resource.

The key issues involved in wilderness water rights have been succinctly reviewed by Meyer (1989). Previously, federal courts have interpreted congressional bills that reserved federal lands (for example, wildlife refuges, Indian reservations) to mean that sufficient quantities of water must be maintained for the purposes of these source lands. This interpretation is contradictory to the understanding many have of western water law, which argues that rights to water are obtained by diverting it to a "beneficial use." Such usage may be defined simply as taking it before someone else does. Downstream consumers fear that reserving water rights for upstream federal lands will endanger their rights and prevent new diversions from occurring. The courts currently are deliberating whether wilderness areas are entitled to the same water rights as other federal reservations (Meyer 1989).

SOME FINAL THOUGHTS

Because wilderness has unique management problems, the BLM needs to engage in extensive educational and public relations efforts to inform users and all citizens about its organizational goals and policies. An effective education program is vital for the acceptance of any management program (see McCool 1990 for a discussion of this point). Possibly the chief reason for the relative success the Forest Service has experienced in managing its wilderness is that the public has a clear notion of its commitment to such efforts. Unfortunately, the BLM is often perceived as being hostile to the aims of wilderness. How the BLM acquired its negative conservation image is not a simple story. It has been argued that this agency historically has been more responsive to local, commodity-oriented groups than has the Forest Service. Fairfax (1988) critically reviewed these BLM–Forest Service differences.

Nevertheless, the perception of bias needs to be fundamentally changed if the BLM is to be effective as a wilderness managing agency. It recently has been making efforts to be viewed as a wise steward of our natural resources. In 1990, the agency entered into an landmark agreement with the Nature Conservancy, a private environmental organization, to save rare and endangered species on BLM lands. In addition, during 1990, the BLM and Forest Service agreed upon a joint recreational fisheries policy, reflecting an increased commitment by the BLM to enhance fishing opportunities. Such high-profile and far-reaching efforts should help the BLM to gain the trust of those interested in wilderness and natural resource conservation.

To attain the greatest success in managing wilderness areas in arid lands, the BLM, other federal and state agencies, and private landowners must improve their coordination and cooperation (Salwasser et al. 1987, Salwasser 1988, Grumbine 1990). All natural areas should be managed in this context: the policies of management agencies must contribute to biodiversity and protect other values inherent in entire ecosystems. Such areas should not be managed as isolated entities.

A tremendous amount of research and planning is yet needed for management policies and practices to be developed and become effective. With so many decisions affecting the composition of these wildernesses still unresolved, it remains to be seen what direction such efforts will take. Hopefully, the chapters herein will suggest wise avenues for policymakers and resource managers.

REFERENCES

Aguirre, G., and M. E. Maury. 1988. "The Mapimi Biosphere, Durango, Mexico." In E. E. Whitehead, C. F. Hutchinson, B. N. Timmerman, and R. G. Varady (eds.) *Arid Lands, Today and Tomorrow*. Proceedings of an international research and development conference. Boulder, Colo.: Westview Press, pp. 223–231.

Allen, E. B. (ed.) 1988. *The Reconstruction of Disturbed Arid Lands, an Ecological Approach.* American Association for the Advancement of Science Selected Symposium 109. Boulder, Colo.: Westview Press.

Ashenfelter, B. 1990. SCLDF docket. *Utah Sierran* 23(3):2.

Bainbridge, B. 1984. "Management Objectives and Goals for Wilderness Areas: Wilderness Areas as a Conservation Category." In V. Martin and M. Inglis (eds.) *Wilderness, the Way Ahead.* Forres, Scotland: Findhorn Press, pp. 114–124.

Baldwin, D. N. 1967. "Wilderness: Concept and Challenge." *Colorado Magazine* 44:224–240.

Battisse, M. 1988. "Progress and Perspectives: A Look Back at UNESCO Arid Zone Activities." In E. E. Whitehead, C. F. Hutchinson, B. N. Timmerman, and R. G. Varady (eds.) *Arid Lands, Today and Tomorrow*. Proceedings of an international research and development conference. Boulder, Colo.: Westview Press, pp. 21–30.

Bonnicksen, T. 1990. "Restoring Biodiversity in Park and Wilderness Areas: An Assessment of the Yellowstone Fires." In A. Rasmussen (ed.) *Wilderness Areas: Their Impacts.* Proceedings of a symposium. Logan, Utah: Cooperative Extension Service, Utah State University, pp. 25–32.

Burford, R. F. 1987. "Managing our Wilderness Heritage." In R. C. Lucas (comp.) *Proceedings— National Wilderness Research Conference: Issues, State-of-knowledge, Future Directions.* United States Department of Agriculture Forest Service General Technical Report INT-220, pp. 35–38.

Crawford, C. S., and J. R. Gosz. 1986. "Dynamics of Desert Resources and Ecosystem Processes." In N. Polunin (ed.) *Ecosystem Theory and Application.* New York: John Wiley and Sons, pp. 63–88.

Evenari, M. 1981. "Synthesis." In D. W. Goodall and R. A. Perry (eds.) *Arid-Land Ecosystems: Structure, Functioning and Management*, Cambridge, U.K.: Cambridge University Press, Vol. 2, pp. 555–591.

Fairfax, S. K. 1988. "The Differences between BLM and the Forest Service." In J. Muhn and H. R. Stuart. *Opportunity and Challenge, the Story of BLM.* Washington, D.C.: Bureau of Land Management, United States Department of the Interior, U.S. Government Printing Office, pp. 226–227.

Fege, A. S. 1990. "Wilderness Management from the National Perspective." Paper presented at the Second North American Interdisciplinary Wilderness Conference, Weber State College, Ogden, Utah.

Flader, S. L. 1978. *Thinking Like a Mountain, Aldo Leopold and the Evolution of an Ecological Attitude Toward Deer, Wolves, and Forests.* Lincoln: University of Nebraska Press.

Franklin, J. F. 1978. "Wilderness Ecosystems." In J. C. Hendee, G. H. Stankey, and R. C. Lucas (eds.) *Wilderness Management.* Washington, D.C.: United States Department of Agriculture Forest Service Miscellaneous Publication No. 1365, U.S. Government Printing Office, pp. 191–211.

González-Romero, A., P. Galina-Tessaro, and S. Alvarez-Cárdenas. 1988. "Wild Bighorn Sheep and Pronghorn Antelope in the Pinacate, Sonora: A Dwindling Resource." In E. E. Whitehead, C. F. Hutchinson, B. N. Timmerman, and R. G. Varady (eds.) *Arid Lands, Today and Tomorrow.* Proceedings of an international research and development conference. Boulder, Colo.: Westview Press, pp. 233–242.

Goudie, A., and J. Wilkinson. 1977. *The Warm Desert Environment.* Cambridge, U.K.: Cambridge University Press.

Gregg, F. 1988. "Implementing FLPMA." In J. Muhn and H. R. Stuart. *Opportunity and Challenge, the Story of BLM.* Washington, D.C.: Bureau of Land Management, United States Department of the Interior, U.S. Government Printing Office.

Grumbine, R. E. 1990. "Viable Populations, Reserve Size, and Federal Lands Management: A Critique." *Conservation Biology* 4:127–134.

Johnson, D. A. 1989. "From Hence We Began . . ." *The Leader* (National Wildlife Federation) 10(9):8.

Johnson, D. R., and J. K. Agee. 1988. "Introduction to Ecosystem Management." In J. K. Agee and D. R. Johnson (eds.) *Ecosystem Management for Parks and Wilderness.* Seattle: University of Washington Press, pp. 3–14.

Ledec, G., and R. Goodland. 1988. *Wildlands, Their Protection and Management in Economic Development.* Washington, D.C.: The World Bank.

Lucas, R. C. 1987. "Perspectives on the History of Wilderness Research." In R. C. Lucas (comp.) *Proceedings—National Wilderness Research Conference: Issues, State-of-knowledge, Future Directions.* United States Department of Agriculture Forest Service General Technical Report INT-220, pp. 15–28.

MacMahon, J. A. 1981. "Introduction." In D. W. Goodall and R. A. Perry (eds.) *Arid-land Ecosystems: Structure, Functioning and Management*, vol. 2. Cambridge, U.K.: Cambridge University Press, pp. 263–269.

Mattox, S. 1990. "Military Goes to War on Public Lands." *The Leader* (National Wildlife Federation) 11(2):6–7.

McCool, S. F. 1990. "Protecting America's Precious Places." In A. Rasmussen (ed.) *Wilderness Areas: Their Impacts.* Proceedings of a symposium. Logan, Utah: Cooperative Extension Service, Utah State University, pp. 1–7.

McGinnies, W. G. 1988. "Climatic and Biological Classifications of Arid Lands: A Comparison." In E. E. Whitehead, C. F. Hutchinson, B. N. Timmerman, and R. G. Varady (eds.) *Arid Lands, Today and Tomorrow.* Proceedings of an international research and development conference. Boulder, Colo.: Westview Press, pp. 61–68.

Mealey, S. P. 1988. "U.S. Forest Service Wilderness Management: Challenge and Opportunity." In J. K. Agee and D. R. Johnson (eds.) *Ecosystem Management for Parks and Wilderness.* Seattle: University of Washington Press, pp. 193–215.

Meyer, C. H. 1989. "A Wilderness Water Rights Compromise." *The Leader* (National Wildlife Federation) 10(9):12.

Muhn, J., and H. R. Stuart. 1988. *Opportunity and Challenge, the Story of BLM.* Washington, D.C.: Bureau of Land Management, United States Department of the Interior, U.S. Government Printing Office.

Porter, D. E. 1987. "New Challenges for Wilderness Research." In R. C. Lucas (comp.) *Proceedings—National Wilderness Research Conference: Issues, State-of-knowledge, Future Directions.* United States Department of Agriculture Forest Service General Technical Report INT-220, pp. 361–362.

Salwasser, H. 1987. "Spotted Owls: Turning a Battleground into a Blueprint." *Ecology* 68:776–779.
———. 1988. "Managing Ecosystems for Viable Populations of Vertebrates: A Focus for Biodiversity." In J. K. Agee and D. R. Johnson (eds.) *Ecosystem Management for Parks and Wilderness*. Seattle: University of Washington Press, pp. 87–104.
Schreiber, R. K., and J. R. Newman. 1987. "Air Quality in Wilderness: A State-of-knowledge Review." In R. C. Lucas (comp.) *Proceedings—National Wilderness Research Conference: Issues, State-of-knowledge, Future Directions*. United States Department of Agriculture Forest Service General Technical Report INT-220, pp. 104–134.
Stankey, G. H., D. N. Cole, R. C. Lucas, M. E. Peterson, and S. S. Frissell. 1985. *The Limits of Acceptable Change (LAC) System for Wilderness Planning*. United States Department of Agriculture Forest Service General Technical Report INT-176.
Starkey, E. E., and G. L. Larson. 1987. "Fish and Wildlife Research and Wilderness in the United States: A State-of-knowledge Review." In R. C. Lucas (comp.) *Proceedings—National Wilderness Research Conference: Issues, State-of-knowledge, Future Directions*. United States Department of Agriculture Forest Service General Technical Report INT-220, pp. 178–190.
Thayn, G. F. 1988. "Wilderness Review Process in Utah." In J. Muhn and H. R. Stuart *Opportunity and Challenge, the Story of BLM*. Washington, D.C.: Bureau of Land Management, United States Department of the Interior, U.S. Government Printing Office, p. 256.
Torres, H., and R. Rodríguez. 1988. "Conservation for Sustainable Development: The Case of the Pampa del Tamarugal National Reserve in the Atacama Desert in Chile." In E. E. Whitehead, C. F. Hutchinson, B. N. Timmerman, and R. G. Varady (eds.) *Arid Lands, Today and Tomorrow*. Proceedings of an international research and development conference. Boulder, Colo.: Westview Press, pp. 1269–1275.
U.S. News and World Report. 1989. "The Battle for the Wilderness." 107(1):16–25.
Watkins, T. H. 1989. "The 'Leftover Lands' Wilderness Battle." *The Leader* (National Wildlife Federation) 10(9):10–11.
Whitehead, E. E., C. F. Hutchinson, B. N. Timmerman, and R. G. Varady (eds.) 1988. *Arid Lands, Today and Tomorrow*. Proceedings of an international research and development conference. Boulder, Colo.: Westview Press.
Wilson, E. O. (ed.) 1988. *BioDiversity*. Washington, D.C.: National Academy Press.

2

IS PRESERVATION OF UTAH'S REMAINING WILDERNESS IN UTAH'S BEST INTEREST?

Wayne Owens

My introduction of the Utah Bureau of Land Management (BLM) Wilderness Act of 1989, the U.S. House of Representatives proposal H.R. 1500, has launched one of the most important Utah public debates of this decade. It necessarily requires a comprehensive reanalysis of our values, our economy, our environmental ethic, our image as a state, and ultimately our sense of obligation to unborn generations and the world community of which we are a part.

Since introduction of H.R. 1500, I have been inundated with calls and letters from people throughout Utah and the country expressing enthusiastic support—some even praising Deity. At the same time, others have claimed that such a large amount of wilderness would:

1. economically hurt the people of southern Utah
2. "lock up the state"
3. halt the state's oil, gas, and mineral development
4. discriminate against handicapped, elderly, and ORV users, in favor of backpackers
5. improperly interfere with the administrative processes of the BLM, and
6. promote environmental "extremism" in a manner "cruelly out of touch" with the people of Utah

It was clear from the beginning that my proposal to preserve Utah's remaining wildlands would spark opposition. I had hoped the debate could center on specific conflicts and a weighing of competing values and opportunities in the context of Utah's modern society. Thus far I have been disappointed. The antiwilderness rhetoric has been composed of sweeping generalizations, most of which are either untrue or grossly exaggerated. This opposition strategy is born of misinformation, or perhaps designed to influence a Utah public assumed to be both naive and shortsighted.

Utahans are not naive, nor are most of them dominated by a desire to exploit short-term economic gains.

I am challenged by the antiwilderness strategy and anxious to present the case for wilderness. The facts, studies, and rationale that can be marshaled are more than adequately responsive; they present a compelling case for preserving Utah's irreplaceable and last-remaining wilderness.

1. WILL DESIGNATION OF LARGE WILDERNESS AREAS HURT THE ECONOMY OF SOUTHERN UTAH?

In January 1986, anticipating this and other wilderness questions, Utah Governor Norman Bangerter charged a multiagency Resource Development Coordinating Committee to prepare a comprehensive technical assessment and wilderness impact report (the "Bangerter Report"). The report was completed and made public as a draft on July 22, 1986 (Utah Governor's Office, 1986.)

The governor's task force began the analysis of this economic question by formulating a baseline projection for employment in southern Utah—wilderness issues and impacts aside. The report concluded:

1. Employment provided by *agriculture* is rapidly declining. "They now comprise only 11 percent and are projected to comprise only 5% of all jobs in the year 2010."
2. "The *oil and gas* industry is not projected to increase its share of total jobs."
3. By 2010, *coal mining* jobs will have increased by only 24.2% over 1982 levels.
4. *Uranium and metal mining* will "remain fairly constant throughout the 1990s and then experience a *slow to moderate growth* through 2010."
5. *Tourism* on the other hand, "*is expected to increase to 40.5% of the total jobs in Southern Utah.*" (More complete quotations from the Bangerter Report are provided in the Appendix.)

The Bangerter task force then addressed the question of what impact, if any, designation of the BLM's wilderness recommendation (two million acres) would have on the state's baseline employment projections for southern Utah.

The report concludes that two million acres of wilderness can be designated with no significant adverse impact. In fact, the reverse is true. It suggests that two million acres of federal wilderness is likely to *increase* employment in the trade and service industries (see the Appendix for quotations of specific findings).

The Bangerter Report also concludes that designation of the BLM proposed two million acres would not impact significantly state mineral-lease revenues of school land income.

The basic economic conclusions of the BLM's Environmental Impact Statement (United States Department of the Interior 1986), which was almost ten years in the making, are essentially the same: "*it is unlikely that exploration*

*or development would occur in most wilderness study areas [3.2 million acres]
even without wilderness designation."*

It is important to realize that the governor's wilderness task force employed
an entirely different approach to conflict analysis than that applied by the
BLM in its study. The BLM relied on experts, resource data, and a public
information gathering process, and then proceeded to eliminate every area
of conflict. The governor's task force also employed experts and the state's
best resource data, but concluded that bias in the analysis could not be
eliminated. The problem was solved by building in both bias and corresponding
balance.

Advocacy teams from six different perspectives were formed to analyze both
wilderness values and potential conflicts. The interests represented by advocacy
teams were:

1. Wilderness values
2. Mineral and energy resources
3. Livestock–Agriculture
4. Land use plans and controls
5. Socioeconomic
6. Wildlife

While the approaches of the BLM and state were significantly different,
the objectives of the studies were much the same—to identify a *common
denominator* of preservable wilderness. *In almost no case were wilderness
values given primacy or permitted to outweigh directly competing economic
values.* Potential wilderness areas in which resource conflicts were identified
were simply eliminated by the BLM or given low possibility rankings in the
case of the Bangerter Report.

Thus, both reports are unfortunately premised on the assumption that the
public desires to preserve wilderness only if it can be done without any significant conflict with potential development.

Notwithstanding this assumption, both the BLM and Bangerter reports
indicate that almost two million acres of BLM wilderness can be preserved
without any economic conflicts of significance.

Among Utah's remaining wildlands (included in H.R. 1500), 1.9 million acres
were not considered by either study. Undoubtedly, there are additional lands
for which no legitimate development conflict can be substantiated.

The BLM and Bangerter reports, given the conservative nature of the analyses employed, have established a "consensus" starting point of approximately
two million acres. The political and legislative task now before us is to do
what these agencies have not yet done: finish the intensive study of all wildlands
improperly excluded from wilderness consideration (1.9 million acres), and
then weigh, through a public and political process, wilderness and compet-

ing values for the three million acres outside the "no-conflict" common denominator that has been identified by both the state and BLM.

A Specific Response to Grazing in Wilderness

The Bangerter Report notes that "existing levels of grazing can continue after wilderness designation" but that ranchers are concerned that management in official wilderness will be more difficult. The problem is more perception than reality.

Rancher's fears are exaggerated and reflect a lack of awareness of the lengthy and special provisions federal wilderness laws and regulations make for livestock use. The 1964 Wilderness Act states that grazing in wilderness areas, if established prior to designation, "shall be permitted to continue subject to such reasonable regulations as are deemed necessary by the Secretary." To clarify any ambiguity as to its intent, Congress has further provided:

> There shall be no curtailment of grazing in wilderness areas simply because an area is, or has been designated as wilderness. *Nor should wilderness designations be used as an excuse by administrators to slowly "phase out" grazing.* Any adjustment in the numbers of livestock permitted to graze in wilderness areas should be made as a result of revisions in the normal grazing and land management planning and policy setting process, giving consideration to legal mandates, range condition, and the protection of the range resource from deterioration.
>
> *The maintenance of supporting facilities,* existing in an area prior to its classification as wilderness (including fences, line cabins, water wells and lines, stock tanks, etc.), *is permissible in wilderness. Where practical alternatives do not exist, maintenance or other activities may be accomplished through the occasional use of motorized equipment.* This may include, for example, the use of backhoes to maintain stock ponds, pickup trucks for major fence repairs, or specialized equipment to repair stock watering facilities. Such occasional use of motorized equipment should be expressly authorized in the grazing permits for the area involved. The use of motorized equipment should be based on a rule of practical necessity and reasonableness. [emphases added]

Federal wilderness grazing regulations set forth twelve factors to be considered in determining "practical necessity and reasonableness." They begin with a charge to minimize threats to private property—which includes provision for emergency stock care—and conclude with a requirement that the age and health of the permittee be considered. *All that is asked is that motorized access be limited to the truly necessary and coordinated so as to minimize the impact on wilderness values.* (It should be noted that wilderness laws make similar provision for private property inholdings and mineral right holders with valid preexisting rights.)

According to the BLM, there are approximately 322 individuals who have grazing privileges within Utah's BLM Wilderness Study Areas (WSAs) (3.2 million acres) being considered for wilderness. For many of them, the amount of their grazing in wilderness is only a minor percentage of the total forage supply they rely upon.

It should not be forgotten that the opportunity to graze livestock on public land is a "privilege." Further, enormous legislative exercise has already been applied to ensure that these privileges can continue in federal wilderness. Is it too much to ask that livestock operators coordinate their management needs with wilderness managing agencies and adjust their privileged use to accommodate the public's expressed desire to preserve remaining wilderness?

The economic benefits of preserving wilderness have been ignored!

Thus far, little attention has been paid to the potential economic benefits of having wilderness. A strong positive case can be made from both economic studies and the actual experience of rural communities near existing federal wilderness areas.

In 1987, the University of Idaho published a study entitled *How Important Is Wilderness? Attitudes of Migrants and Residents in Wilderness Counties* (Rudzitis 1987). The study contrasts the growth of rural counties that contain or are adjacent to federal wilderness with the growth of nonwilderness rural counties. The study found that

> *Counties which contain or are adjacent to a federally designated wilderness are among the fastest growing in the United States . . .* these largely rural remote areas grew at a rate of 30 percent or double the 15 percent rate of growth for non-metropolitan areas as a whole. [emphases added]

This finding was supplemented by another:

> Younger highly educated migrants are the most important components of the inflow into these counties. Over 74 percent either had some college, or completed graduate work . . . economic reasons were not the main reasons why people moved to these counties. Non-economic amenity reasons (outdoor recreation, landscape, pace of life, environmental quality) were more important than factors such as employment opportunity . . . the majority of migrants either had no change in income or suffered a loss in income . . . *The presence of wilderness was a very important reason why people moved to or stay in these counties . . .*
>
> On the question of whether wilderness should be open for development, they felt strongly (83 to 94 percent) that it should not. An even larger number (91 to 98 percent) felt that nearby wilderness areas were important to their county. [emphases added]

The study references thirty other related studies as corroborative.

Encouraged by this Idaho study, I have started an informal survey of the experience and opinions of mayors, county commissioners, and civic leaders in western rural communities near wilderness. On May 17, 1989, I received an enthusiastic letter response from the mayor of Santa Fe, New Mexico. He reports:

> In response to your request, *our experiences in Santa Fe have proven that economic growth is definitely enhanced by our proximity to adjacent National Forest and wilderness areas* . . .
>
> Wilderness areas add much to the "quality of life" elements of the region which help to draw new industry to the area. These elements will become more important in the future as more "footloose" high-tech industries decide to relocate to relatively uncrowded urban areas . . .

Last year, Mayor Lawrence J. Young of Ketchum, Idaho, testified to the Senate Energy and Natural Resources Committee that his community wanted more wilderness than was being recommended by the Forest Service. His testimony reads:

> Resolution Number 357 was passed unanimously by the Ketchum City Council with strong support from the business community, the Ketchum–Sun Valley Chamber of Commerce and local environmental groups. That Resolution states, in part:
>
> > Wilderness designation (with acreage similar to those proposed by H.R. 1512) for the areas commonly referred to as the Pioneers, the Smoky Mountains, the Boulder/White Clouds and Sawtooth Completion is *an integral part of the near and long term economic plan for the City of Ketchum.*
> >
> > . . . Congress has an opportunity to provide Ketchum-Sun Valley with *an attraction unparalleled in the United States* . . .
>
> Wilderness designation for areas surrounding Ketchum–Sun Valley . . . comparable to the acreage proposed in H.R. 1512 will provide Ketchum, with *bold marketing options that will translate into jobs and increased local and state tax revenues. Ketchum is strongly opposed to the Idaho Forest Management Plan S. 2055.* [emphases added]

On June 1, 1989, I received a letter from the Sun Valley–Ketchum Chamber of Commerce. The closing paragraph states:

> Last year the Sun Valley–Ketchum Chamber of Commerce testified against the McClure/Andrus Wilderness Proposal because there was *not enough* federally designated wilderness proposed for our area. *We have the potential to market our community as a wilderness mecca just as you do in Utah.* Our experience has convinced us that the wilderness which surrounds us, some of it federally preserved (and we are lobbying for more in the future), is a major economic resource and a *keystone to future economic growth.* [emphases added]

The Chamber of Commerce and civic leaders of Grants, New Mexico, a small rural community undertook a similar prowilderness campaign to support creation of the El Malpais National Monument.

Aspen, Colorado, whose summer tourism traffic is lured primarily by surrounding wilderness attractions, is another reported economic success attributed, at least in part, to an abundance of federally designated wilderness.

On June 9, 1989, I had the opportunity to chair a hearing in Phoenix on proposals for BLM wilderness in Arizona. Led by statements of the governor and the mayor of Phoenix, witness after witness testified for the larger of the two wilderness proposals. They argued that preserving Arizona's remaining wilderness was key to their state's economic vitality, image, and quality of life.

In virtually all of the states that surround us, political and civic leaders alike not only recognize the economic and aesthetic value of wilderness, but actively seek to promote it. The contrast with currently expressed attitudes of Utah's leaders is distressingly apparent.

I recently received an interesting pilot study conducted by an energetic group of Moab residents. A questionnaire was sent to approximately 330 people who had inquired of Moab's Chamber of Commerce about relocating to or visiting Moab. The questionnaire asked them to rate how different economic activities and quality-of-life considerations would effect Moab's attractiveness as a place to live or visit. The methodology was based on recommendations from experts at Utah State University, UCLA, and Mesa College. *Ninety percent (90%) of the respondents saw that access to quality wilderness was a major attraction.* Expansion of extractive industry development was perceived as a significant negative.

These kinds of reports are not news to those in Utah. I noticed that a brochure, recently developed by Cache County to lure new "high tech" business, features a backpacker hiking on a trail in the Mt. Naomi Wilderness Area. The message of our Olympics promotional campaign is unmistakable: "Utah is beautiful and pristine. We take care of it and we will take care of you." To summarize, *there is no evidence that the BLM's conservative two million acre wilderness proposal would economically harm the state or southern Utah.* A close examination of the BLM and Bangerter reports suggests that this two million acre figure could be greatly increased with no adverse affect. In fact, *there is substantial evidence that progressive federal wilderness designations may indeed be the single most important economic opportunity available to southern Utah,* as well as a critically important component of the image we are building to serve our future.

2. WOULD PASSAGE OF H.R. 1500 LOCK UP THE STATE?

Utah's land area is approximately 54,346,440 acres. Of that, 1,737,057 acres have been set aside as national parks, monuments, or recreation areas. There are 2,751,000 acres of defense or other federal withdrawals. Approximately 900,000 acres of Forest Service lands have been designated as official wilderness. If we add to that the 5 million acres that H.R. 1500 proposes to preserve (9% of the state) as wilderness, there still would be more than 43,958,383 acres (81%) open to development.

The charge that passage of H.R. 1500 would "lock up the state" is clearly a gross exaggeration.

3. WOULD PASSAGE OF H.R. 1500 STOP THE STATE'S OIL, GAS AND MINERAL DEVELOPMENT?

The Bangerter Report states:

> The Uintah Basin, which includes the largest share of Utah's oil and gas industry, as well as much of the tar sands resource, was not included in this analysis because under the proposed action [2 million acres] no WSAs in Uintah County were included. It is unlikely that any area in the Uintah Basin would be impacted by BLM wilderness designation.

Both the BLM and Bangerter reports acknowledge that only 12% of the state's proven or indicated oil and gas reserves lay within the 3.2 million acres of BLM WSAs. Only 346,480 of the 1.9 million acres added for wilderness consideration by H.R. 1500 lay within the Uintah Basin.

A precise estimate of the oil and gas reserves that lay under this additional 1.9 million acres is not yet available. If, for the sake of argument, however, the reserves under the BLMs 3.2 million acres of WSAs is increased 38% (1.9 = 38% of 5 million), and further assuming that the full 5 million acres of H.R. 1500 are designated wilderness, 83% of the state's known and indicated reserves would still remain available for development.

The BLM and Bangerter reports agree that the coal reserves under the BLM proposed 2 million acres are approximately 2% of the state's known reserves. According to the Bangerter Report, we have mined little more than 2% of the state's total coal reserve since the beginning of Utah's coal mining history. Even if the potential coal mining conflicts identified in the BLM and Bangerter reports are doubled, they cannot be argued credibly as presenting any significant conflict.

Fortunately, our state has an almost unlimited supply of coal in areas where most of the state's coal development has and will continue to occur even if House Resolution 1500 becomes law. No real conflict exists between wilderness proposed by H.R. 1500 and the coal industry's need in Emery, Carbon, and Sanpete counties.

The analysis is much the same for tar sands, uranium, and metal mining. The reserves that would be foregone are minimal in the context of the state's total reserves, and the prospects for any near-term development, according to the State Planning Office, are low in any case. According to this office, projections for mining industry growth in the affected areas are moderate at best. (See the Bangerter Report for further details.)

Why is it that the fossil fuel and mineral reserves under these wildlands have remained undeveloped? Very simply, it is because these deposits lay in remote areas that are very costly to develop. Far easier, more economically extractable mineral resources are available, enough to last for centuries, within lands unaffected by H.R. 1500, and should the minerals in the lands proposed by H.R. 1500 ever be needed, their wilderness designation could be altered by Congress.

Clearly, the charge of harm to important natural resource development opportunities is grossly inaccurate, even if all of the five million acres proposed by H.R. 1500 are preserved.

4. DOES H.R. 1500 DISCRIMINATE AGAINST HANDICAPPED, ELDERLY, AND ORV USERS IN FAVOR OF BACKPACKERS?

House Resolution 1500 has been endorsed by S'PLORE, an organization dedicated entirely to assisting handicapped people to experience outdoor recreation and the natural environment. Their endorsement speaks for itself.

I have received a number of letters and calls from senior citizens commending the introduction of H.R. 1500. I was particularly affected by one, which I think is representative, from Mrs. Mildred Breedlove of Ferron, Utah. It opens:

> Dear Congressman Owens:
>   Your stand on wildlife and wilderness pleases me greatly. I would like to help in this battle . . .

The letter goes on to tell of the satisfaction she finds in knowing we have undertaken to ensure that a portion of Utah will be preserved, untrammeled by man, for her descendants and generations to come. The letter closes:

> P.S. I will be 85 years old next month, not much time left.

I'm sure she will never walk, or probably even see, most of the acres in H.R. 1500. Yet their preservation holds great importance for her. To Mrs. Breedlove, joining in the battle for H.R. 1500 represents an unselfish act and an expression of reverence for natural beauty.

I was similarly impressed by the testimony of a senior citizen in the recent Arizona BLM wilderness hearings I chaired. She spoke on behalf of the Sun City Retirement Community Home Owners Association. When asked why so many seniors were supporting the largest wilderness bill being proposed in Arizona, she simply answered; "We love to walk, but, we are doing this for our children and grandchildren."

The wilderness proposed by H.R. 1500 is already divided into more than sixty units, separated, and in many cases surrounded by roads or public access corridors. It is already contemplated that H.R. 1500 would permit a score of one-hundred-foot-wide "cherry stems" into wilderness areas, to preserve most presently existing and frequently used roads.

In contrast to the great wildernesses of Idaho, Montana, and Alaska, there are a few places within H.R. 1500 where you can get more than five miles from a road. There are no places where you can get more than seven air miles from a point of public access. In fact, with the exception of canyon bottoms, almost all areas within H.R. 1500 can be seen from a vista to which a car or ORV can be driven.

As demand for quality outdoor recreation increases, as it surely will, our forests and wilderness areas will become more crowded. In the recent Arizona hearings, the governor's statement indicated that dispersed recreation (principally hiking and backpacking) now represents 68% of the outdoor recreation on public lands in Arizona. Nothing makes a wild area seem smaller than motorized vehicles that can cover hundreds of miles in a day.

Over forty years ago Aldo Leopold (1949) addressed the arguments for all-inclusive vehicular access, and his response could not be more timely today. He submitted:

> There are those who decry wilderness sports as undemocratic because the recreational carrying capacity of a wilderness is small, as compared with a golf links or a tourist camp. The basic error in such argument is what is intended to counteract mass production. The value of recreation is not a matter of ciphers. Recreation is valuable in proportion to the intensity of its experiences, and to the degree to which it differs from and contrasts with a workaday life. By these criteria, mechanized outings are at best a milk-and-water affair.
>
> Mechanized recreation already has seized nine tenths of the woods and mountains; a decent respect for minorities [and I would add: a spiritual reverence for the naturalness of the earth] *should dedicate the other tenth to wilderness.* [emphasis added]

H.R. 1500 would make that long overdue commitment to preserve one tenth of our state as a kind of natural tithe.

5. DOES H.R. 1500 IMPROPERLY DISREGARD THE
ADMINISTRATIVE PROCESS OF THE BLM?

An appreciation for the history of the BLM is key to understanding the need for H.R. 1500. The BLM was the offspring of President Truman's decision to combine a government land disposal agency with the Federal Grazing Service. Predictably, the resulting hybrid was best at two things: disposing of public resources and providing grazing.

In the 1960s America awakened to the value of its public lands. Under the leadership of President John Kennedy and Secretary of the Interior Stewart L. Udall, the BLM began a transformation into an agency with a broader public mission. In 1964, federal Multiple Use and Wilderness acts were passed. From that date until the election of President Reagan, thanks in large part to the efforts of supportive administrations and passage of key environmental laws (that is, those supported by the National Environmental Policy Act and the environmental movement), the balance of BLM management policies steadily improved.

Between the passage of the Federal Land Management and Policy Act (FLPMA) in 1976 and the end of the Carter administration, the BLM's budget and staff nearly doubled, with increases in all areas including wilderness stewardship. In 1981, a study from the John Hopkins University Press could report that while a bias still existed, the BLM was no longer a captive of grazing and commodity interests.

The FLPMA mandated in 1976 that the BLM conduct an inventory of all remaining wilderness, to be followed by a recommendation to Congress concerning the areas suitable for official wilderness designation. The recommendation was to be guided by the definition of *wilderness* as set forth in the Wilderness Act of 1964. Every party or interest who intends to participate in this Utah wilderness decision should be familiar with the Wilderness Act's expression of our national desire to preserve wilderness:

A wilderness, in contrast with those areas where man and his own works dominate the landscape, is hereby recognized as an area where the earth and its community of life are untrammeled by man, where man himself is a visitor who does not remain. An area of wilderness is further defined to mean in this Act an area of undeveloped Federal land retaining its primeval character and influence, *without permanent improvements or human habitation*, which is protected and managed so as to preserve its natural conditions and which (1) generally appears to have been affected primarily by the forces of nature, with the imprint of man's work substantially unnoticeable; (2) has outstanding opportunities for solitude or a primitive and unconfined type of recreation; (3) has at least five thousand acres of land or is of sufficient size as to make practicable its preservation and use in an unimpaired condition; and (4) may also contain ecological, geological, or other features of scientific, educational, scenic, or historical values.[1]

After almost two decades of gains under five presidents, environmentalists were stunned in 1981 when the new Secretary of the Interior, James Watt, characterized their goals as "extremist" and announced that the Reagan administration intended to "reverse twenty-five years of bad resource management." The knee-jerk assumption, that every environmental gain would burden the economy with a corresponding loss for business, developed overnight in the new administration.

By attempting to phase out programs like the Land and Water Conservation Fund, Secretary of the Interior James Watt and his successor succeeded in adding fewer lands to America's national parks, monuments, and refuges than any administration in history.

During the eight years of the Reagan administration, the Department of Interior sold more public domain and leased more federal land for energy development than the preceding Carter, Ford, Nixon, and Johnson administrations combined.

After 1981, much of the best legal talent in the environmental movement was being applied to compel Secretary Watt and other Reagan appointees to faithfully execute existing environmental laws and to fight off initiatives such as the "Sage Brush Rebellion."

In 1985, Anne M. Burford, Reagan's first EPA administrator, resigned amidst turmoil resulting, in part, from her public statement that: "the Administration has no commitment to the environment and no environmental policy."

Former Secretary of the Interior Stewart L. Udall, a founding father to many of our nation's environmental policies, summarizes the impact of the Reagan years in his recent edition of *The Quiet Crisis* (1988):

> It is clear that on environmental issues Ronald Reagan rowed against the American mainstream for eight years. The "great communicator" was unable to persuade Congress to repeal a single important law he disliked. *He is the only president this century who served his term without proposing any major initiative to further the cause of conservation.*

The House Interior Committee, on which I serve, and where Utah's wilderness question is now pending, has spent much of its time working to counter the erosion of environmental sensitivity within the BLM and other federal

---

1. Some say all of H.R. 1500 lands do not qualify because of mines, trails, or old cabins. Pre-existing mineral claims can be grandfathered, eventually, when the claim has been played out, and the land can be reclaimed and qualified, fulfilling the intent behind "without permanent improvements."

agencies. In recent hearings, preparatory to reauthorization of FLPMA legislation, the GAO reported with stunning candor:

> The BLM has not adequately balanced the competing demands on the natural resources that it is mandated to foster, protect, and preserve. The BLM has often placed the needs of commercial interests such as livestock permittees and mine operators ahead of . . . the long-term health of the resources. As a result, some permittees have come to view the use of these lands as a property right for private benefit, rather than a conditional privilege conferred by the public at large.

It was in this atmosphere that the BLM's analysis of Utah's wilderness opportunity developed. In April 1979, the BLM's initial inventory had eliminated seventeen of the twenty-two million acres under review as "clearly and obviously lacking in wilderness quality." Between April 1979 and November 1980, another 2.4 million acres were summarily eliminated, based primarily on speculated development conflicts and the pointed lobbying of local special-interest groups, leaving a decision trail that prompted five years of litigation and congressional oversight investigations.

In response to the November 1980 wilderness eliminations, angry conservation groups challenged decisions concerning almost one million acres. Their fourteen-hundred-page brief presented the most comprehensive appeal ever filed before the Interior Board of Land Appeals (IBLA).

In April 1983, with a shocking indictment of the BLM's analysis, the IBLA ordered a reinventory of 88% of the acres under appeal. The BLM begrudgingly completed the IBLA-demanded reinventory and added 560,000 acres to study status. The conservationists again appealed; this time the concern was over 225,000 acres that were reinventoried but not added. In April 1985 the IBLA again found the BLM in error and ordered that 77,000 acres in the Henry Mountains be added for study.

Beginning in 1983, charges of mismanagement brought House Public Lands Subcommittee Chairman Rep. John Seiberling (D, Ohio) on a fact-finding mission to Utah. He returned to Washington convinced that discretion had been abused: "They've left out areas that obviously qualify for wilderness— and I've seen a lot of them . . . I mean, their position is absolutely absurd," he told Utah reporters.

In 1984 and 1985 a series of congressional oversight hearings were held to investigate the problems. The investigations identified scores of inventory abuses and foreordained the attitude that Congress would have toward the agencies' ultimate recommendation.

Preservation of Utah's remaining wilderness is fast becoming one of the top five national conservation causes. Following my introduction of H.R. 1500, the entire leadership of the House Interior Committee joined in a letter to Secretary of the Interior Manuel Lujan, restating their criticisms of the inventory process and requesting that the BLM protect all lands proposed by H.R. 1500, so as to preserve the prerogatives of Congress to evaluate the wilderness opportunity on Utah's federal lands.

It is my estimation that Congress would not pass the BLM's two-million-acre wilderness proposal even if it was supported by the entire Utah delegation. Rather, Congress would likely wait, leaving intact "Wilderness Study Area" protection for at least 3.2 million acres until a more progressive proposal could be formulated.

Many of the BLM's exclusions from wilderness consideration are patently indefensible. On the southern perimeter of the San Rafael Swell, some eighty thousand acres of the Muddy Creek wilderness were eliminated by the adoption of a roadless county line for a boundary.

In defense of another exclusion, the BLM declared that the spectacular dikes and sills surrounding Little Black Mountain *"do not compare with those in the Cedar Mountain area."* Just one year later, a National Park Service study identified Little Black Mountain as "one of the most instructive and one of the most dramatic, easily seen complexes of igneous intrusions anywhere in the world."

Then, with inconsistent logic, *the Cedar Mountain roadless area was also cut* from the inventory. The BLM concluded that its colorful badlands, volcanic cliffs, and dikes were *"not an outstanding scenic feature when compared with . . . such areas as . . . San Rafael Knob."* Then, with consistent inconsistency, the *San Rafael Knob, too, was cut* from the inventory.

Labyrinth Canyon, a rare place in Utah's desert wilds that offers nearly fifty miles of smooth-water canoeing (the epitome of American wilderness travel), was *illogically delineated by a wilderness boundary that runs right down the center of the river.* This is the wilderness of which John Wesley Powell (1961) wrote:

> There is an exquisite charm in our ride today down this beautiful canyon. It gradually grows deeper with every mile of travel; the walls are symmetrically curved and grandly arched, of a beautiful color, and reflected in the quiet waters. . . .
> We are all in fine spirits and feel very gay, and the badinage of the men is echoed from wall to wall.

A flight over this meandering river corridor, opening to view the immense and untouched wilds on both sides, obviates the loss in limiting our wilderness opportunity to the BLM's framework for consideration.

During the earliest stages of the inventory, the BLM was hounded with requests to eliminate another large block of San Rafael wilderness because of its proximity to a proposed power plant development. The BLM elected to conduct a special accelerated study and, within fourteen months, had cut some 300,000 acres of pristine wilderness from the inventory to provide for a power plant that would never be built.

Clearly, the task of weighing wilderness values against all other competing values associated with Utah's remaining wildlands has not even begun. Wholesale reliance on the BLM's review process and recommendations, which were obviously compromised by the political climate existing at the time and pressure to placate local ranchers and would-be developers, would be a great disservice to our state and future.

Our supply of remaining wilderness is fixed. What we will preserve with this decision is all that will ever be preserved. The natural resources available on the 80% of Utah lands available for development will easily provide more than our needs, far beyond any time relevant to this decision. *Should national emergency require, the Wilderness Act provides for immediate invasion by presidential order. Moreover, Congress can always reverse its decision should justification arise.*

The Bangerter Report contains the believable prediction that the value of wilderness to both Utahans and the nation will steadily increase. If we must err in this decision, let us err on the side of preservation.

6. IS A PROPOSAL LIKE H.R. 1500 "CRUELLY OUT OF TOUCH" WITH THE PEOPLE OF UTAH?

Notwithstanding a decade devoid of presidential leadership on conservation issues, the American people have entered an age of environmental alarm. A Louis Harris poll (1989) reveals an increasing level of concern for the environment and dissatisfaction with the responsiveness of government. These are among its findings:

The American public believes this country's environment is in bad shape, by almost 2 to 1.

The most poignant statements come from older Americans, who can remember the nation before the onslaught of super highways, acid rain and toxic waste; they take a much dimmer view of the environment than the younger generation who has never known such times.

The American public is convinced that the environment is going to be much worse in 50 years than it is now.

An almost unanimous 97% of the American public thinks the country should be doing more to protect the environment and curb pollution.

81% of the American public expressed a willingness to pay higher taxes to protect the environment.

From illustrations that range from overwhelming national support for returning wolves to Yellowstone Park to public outrage expressed over the oil spill in Prince William Sound, it is clear that the American people are developing an increasingly sensitive land ethic.

Studies and polls suggest that this trend is equally true for the people of the Intermountain West. A wilderness study conducted by Colorado State University (Walsh et al. 1981) was reviewed in the Bangerter Report. It found that "84.1 percent of Colorado's population favor protection of wilderness and are willing to pay for wilderness preservation." The study concluded that Colorado households would be willing to pay up to nineteen dollars more annually for the preservation of 2.6 million acres of wilderness. After analyzing the comparable distributions and demographics of Utah and Colorado's population, the governor's report states: "*It seems reasonable to conclude that the results of these Colorado studies are transferable to Utah.*"

A recent Colorado wilderness poll, taken in April 1989, indicated that *Colorado residents favor additional large wilderness designations by a margin of eight to one.* By a margin of three to one, they favored the establishment of wilderness water rights to preserve wild rivers, even if it meant development opportunities would be lost.

Similar studies and polls have been done on the views of Utahans. The summary of a Brigham Young University study, released in May 1987, concludes:

> 86% of the respondents think it is "important" or "very important" to preserve some pristine, unique, natural areas as wilderness in Utah.
>
> . . . *the value of additional wilderness designation remains significantly high up until approximately 8–10 million acres or approximately 15 percent of the state* is preserved. [emphasis added]

The findings of a survey conducted by the University of Utah Survey Research Center, completed in July 1986 and made a part of the Bangerter Report, concluded:

> 83% agreed or strongly agreed that "for adequate protection, environmentally sensitive areas need official designation as wilderness"
>
> 74.5% agreed or strongly agreed that "wilderness designation enhances recreation opportunity in Utah"
>
> 77.6% agreed or strongly agreed that "wilderness designation enhances the image of Utah as a tourism State"

A recent (March 1989) Deseret News/KSL poll found that

> 43% believed that 2 or more million acres should be designated
>
> Of that number, *34% believed 3 or more million acres should be designated*

only 23% believed that 1.9 million acres [essentially the BLM proposal] or less should be designated

Only 1% wanted no more wilderness at all.

When a hefty 34% of Utahans want more than three million acres of wilderness federally designated, is it "cruelly out of touch" and "unreasonable" to propose that at least 5 million acres be protected and considered? It would appear that proposals in the neighborhood of 800 million acres, or even 1.4 million are minority positions. The "extremists" are those advocating no more wilderness at all.

House Resolution 1500 calls for congressional consideration of 5 million acres of Utah BLM wild lands. *It is my hope that we will ultimately designate and preserve at least four million of these acres. That puts me in the middle of the progressive forefront of the Utahans (34%) who are most interested in preserving our environmental heritage and quality of life. That is right where I want to be.*

Every Utah wilderness study or poll to date suggests that H.R. 1500 is the most popular Utah wilderness position yet made public.

CONCLUSION

The responses above present primarily the economic and political case for wilderness. All indications are that these arguments will become stronger over time. In my mind, however, these are not the best or highest reasons for preserving wilderness. I concur with what Henry David Thoreau said: "In wilderness is the preservation of the world." Utah's BLM wildlands may be the last home of at least fifteen threatened or endangered species. They are an uncompromised reservoir of Utah's natural diversity. They are what remains of a resource that was not inherited, but, rather, borrowed from future generations.

Utah's BLM wildlands are unique in all the world. The nation as a whole, co-owners with us of this extraordinary beauty, has already recognized their irreplaceable natural value in establishing seven national parks, monuments, and recreation areas. In response to just one letter from my office, forty-seven members of Congress have already requested the opportunity to cosponsor H.R. 1500—and the list grows daily. The nation now watches closely as we Utahans prepare to express our sense of stewardship for the 10% of Utah that remains as it was originally created.

I believe that many individuals among our state's political leadership are not recognizing the increasing concern for our land and environment that is felt by a majority of Utahans. "No-wilderness" resolutions, maximum development proposals advanced under the banner of "multiple use," and the automatic willingness to put fish and wildlife resources behind commodity-user interests are dangerously out of touch with the majority of Utahans and the true interests of our state.

To my great disappointment, Utah is developing an antienvironmental image. I believe this is spiritually debilitating and potentially an economic disaster. Recently, a report was distributed by the Energy and Commerce Committee's Health and Environment Subcommittee. It was entitled "State of the States," and ranked the fifty states by their order of protection and attitude toward the environment. Utah was ranked forty-eighth.

The conservation voting records of many of Utah political leaders makes a similar disinterested statement. Astonishingly, for some Utah leaders, a poor conservation voting record is considered a bragging point.

After more than two hundred years of "manifest destiny" and the systematic taming of America's wilderness, our nation and most Utahans have come to understand what our Indian predecessors knew from the beginning—that unborn generations have a claim on the land equal to our own and that men need to learn from nature and replenish their spirits through frequent contacts with animals and wildland. Few people are aware of the progressive land ethic continuously underscored by Utah's first governor, Brigham Young. He abhorred waste and taught that honorable stewardship included the preservation of naturalness whenever possible. Early Mormons were counseled to take no more from the lands than their actual needs required.

Utah's BLM wilderness decision will be a statement of our values, our land ethic, and ultimately our commitment, as John Kennedy eloquently said, "to hand down undiminished to those who come after us, the natural wealth and beauty which is ours." My introduction of H.R. 1500 was intended to ensure that our statement will be commensurate with the natural heritage that is ours.

REFERENCES

Harris Poll. 1989. "Public Worried about State of Environment Today and in Future." Harris Poll Brief, release date—14 May. Washington, D.C.: Louis Harris Associates.

Leopold, A. 1949. *A Sand County Almanac and Sketches Here and There*. New York: Oxford University Press.

Powell, J. W. 1961 (reprint). *The Exploration of the Colorado River and Its Canyons*. New York: Dover Publications.

Rudzitis, G. 1987. "How Important is Wilderness: Attitudes of Migrants and Residents in Wilderness Counties." Paper presented at 4th World Wilderness Congress, Estes Park, Colorado. (Published by the University of Idaho, Moscow, Idaho.)

Udall, S. 1988. *The Quiet Crisis and the Next Generation*. New York: Holt, Rinehart and Winston.

United States Department of the Interior. 1986. *Utah BLM Statewide Wilderness Environmental Impact Statement*. Prepared by Utah BLM office, Bureau of Land Management, 6 vols. Washington, D.C.: United States Government Printing Office.

Utah Governor's Office. 1986. "Resource Development Coordinating Committee Wilderness

Subcommittee's Report to Governor Norman H. Bangerter on the Bureau of Land Management's Statewide Wilderness Draft Environmental Impact Statement." Salt Lake City, Utah.

Walsh, R. G., R. A. Gillman, and J. B. Loomis. 1981. *Wilderness Resource Economics: Recreation Use and Preservation Values.* Denver, Colo.: American Wilderness Alliance.

APPENDIX

BASELINE EMPLOYMENT PROJECTIONS FOR SOUTHERN UTAH AS PER THE BANGERTER REPORT:

"AGRICULTURAL related employment, which includes farm proprietors, employees of farms and agricultural service employees, was 7,838 in 1967. In 1985 this employment was 6,340, *a 24 percent decline.* In the year 2010 employment is projected to be 4,998, *a 27 percent decline.* This follows state and national trends. . . . These farm jobs comprised 23 percent of all jobs in 1967. They now comprise only 11 percent and are projected to comprise only *5 percent of all jobs in the year 2020.* . . .

"OIL AND GAS employment in the impacted region [refers to BLM WSAs, 3.2 million acres] in 1967 was 350. The industry peaked in 1981 at 1,061. In 1985 the level of employment had dropped to 567, its lowest level since 1975. . . . Projections using historical trends and national projections for this industry show employment of 1,304 by the year 2010. . . . *The oil and gas industry is not projected to increase its share of total jobs in Southern Utah.* . . .

"COAL mining consisted of 1,258 jobs in 1967 and grew to a peak of 5,089 in 1982. . . . Coal mining declined to a low of 2,785 jobs in 1984 . . . Coal mining under a baseline scenario is projected to reach 6,622 jobs *by 2010, more than doubling today's level, but only 1,600 jobs higher than the 1982 peak.*"

URANIUM AND METAL MINING. "Although employment in Southern Utah for this sector grew rapidly through the later part of the 1970s, growing from 1,008 in 1974 to a high 2,074 in 1979, employment during the 1980s has experienced drastic reductions. . . . The uranium industry nationwide has experienced a similar decline over the same period because of surpluses of uranium supply due to an over estimated demand for nuclear energy in the 1980s and safety concerns about the nuclear power generation. The employment level in the metal mining industry is *projected to remain fairly constant throughout the 1990s and then experience a slow to moderate level of growth through 2010.*"

TOURISM. "All of Southern Utah counties have experienced significant growth in the trade and service industries in the last two decades and are projected to continue to experience this growth through the year 2010. The trade and service industries contain most of the tourist related activities in the region.

"Like the rest of the state, the trade and service industries are projected to increase their proportion of total employment. The continuing decline in the agriculture, mining and manufacturing industries contributes to this trend.

"Total employment in the Southern Utah trade industry in 1967 was 5,523. Ten years later, total employment has increased by 72.9 percent to 9,550. . . . By 2010, employment is projected to be 21,172 or 23.9 percent of total employment.

"Employment in the service industry follows a similar pattern. Service jobs in 1980 made up 10.7 percent of total employment. By 2010 service employment is expected to make up 16.7 percent of total employment.

"*These projections demonstrate that the trade and services will become an increasingly important part of the Southern Utah economy.* . . . By 2010 their share is expected to increase to 40.5 percent."

THE IMPACTS OF TWO MILLION ACRES OF WILDERNESS ON BASELINE EMPLOYMENT PROJECTIONS AS PER THE BANGERTER REPORT:

AGRICULTURE. "Grazing activities are the component of the agricultural industry which is of concern with respect to wilderness. The DEIS [BLM's Draft Environmental Impact Statement] states that existing levels of *grazing can continue after wilderness designation* (no decrease in AUMs). Ranchers are concerned, however, that wilderness will make it more difficult to manage their grazing activities. *If this is true, then there is a possibility that agricultural activities might decline faster than the baseline projections indicate . . . However, it would be difficult to determine whether this impact would exceed the 5 percent criteria* [Utah statutory definition of significant impact] in any community or county."

OIL AND GAS. "It would appear, with known oil and gas reserves, that *the designation of wilderness would not prohibit the achievement of this baseline projection for the year 2010.* . . . For example, the DEIS states that '. . . the projected amount of oil in Utah BLM WSA's (total estimated in-place resource) is less than four-tenths of 1 percent of the projected U.S. proven and indicated reserves and 12 percent of the estimated Utah proven and indicated reserves.' *In other words, it appears we could achieve the baseline projection [of employment] by developing the other 88 percent of Utah's oil reserves.*"

COAL. "According to the Utah Energy Office, between 1890 and 1985, some 467,293,000 tons of coal have been mined in Utah. This is only 2 percent of the known reserves in the state.

"It should be noted that most of the WSAs included in the proposed action contain relatively small coal resources. . . . Some of the WSAs under BLM proposed action, however, do contain marketable coal. The DEIS states '. . . an estimated resource of up to 149.5 million tons of in-place coal reserves in 10 WSAs (72.6 million tons recoverable) would be forgone with this alternative [the BLM proposed action]. This would be *about 2.3% of the estimated in-place coal reserves in Utah.* . . .

"*It would appear that wilderness designation would not prohibit the achievement of the baseline projection.*"

URANIUM AND METAL MINING. "Given the current amount of stockpiled uranium, the slow to moderate projected growth in the metal mining industry and the small amount of reserves located in WSAs, *the likelihood of wilderness designation causing a significant impact to the uranium industry or the local economies involved is very low.*"

TAR SANDS. "The DEIS states that, "overall about 934 million barrels of in-place oil (280.9 million barrels recoverable) from estimated tar sands resources in these WSAs would be forgone. Since this would be only about 2% to 4% of the total estimated 23 to 45 billion barrels of in-place resources in Utah, it would not be a significant loss.

"Because of the small percentage of total reserves located in the WSAs and the apparent downturn in the tar sands industry, *wilderness designation will not likely cause a significant impact in the affected counties.*"

POWER PLANT DEVELOPMENT. "Wilderness is not likely to alter the baseline projection for this industry in this region."

STATE AND LOCAL GOVERNMENT REVENUE IMPACTS. " . . . *the designation of wilderness would not create significant mineral lease revenue impacts statewide and in most counties . . .*" [The report does indicate, using a worst case analysis, that state mineral revenues could go down 1.8 million, but then points out that such a loss would be roughly equivalent to the revenue loss that would follow a two-dollar change in the price of oil.]

SCHOOL LAND INCOME. "If no exchanges were to occur on these lands and leases were relinquished, the State could lose $345,000. . . . This loss would comprise 2.9 percent of school land income. However, State land income comprises only 2.1 percent of the uniform school fund. Therefore, this potential loss in the uniform school fund would equal 0.05 percent (½ of ⅒ of one percent). *Obviously this would be insignificant to the uniform school fund.*"

TOURISM. "*[W]ilderness designation will likely increase total employment in the trade and service sectors in Southern Utah.* However, at this point it is difficult to determine how significant this increase will be."

"In the DEIS, BLM suggests that in many WSAs, visitor days will increase.

They estimate that each visitor will spend $4.10 per day. It should be noted that other studies have shown much higher values for wilderness visitor days. For example, a study conducted by Colorado State University entitled *Wilderness Resource Economics: Recreation Use and Preservation Values*, shows that Colorado residents paid $14.00 per visitor day for wilderness visits."

PROJECTED INCREASE IN THE VALUE OF WILDERNESS IN UTAH:

"Other noted economists (citations omitted) contend that the real economic benefit from preservation of wilderness areas would increase over time compared to the benefits from alternative uses of these lands. This is due to the fact that wilderness environments are fixed in supply while the demand for the recreational use of wilderness continues to rise rapidly. Population growth in the west is expected to continue to grow rapidly and there will be substantial future growth in income and education levels as well as changes in age distributions.

"Alternative forms of recreation will become more crowded and with more leisure time available the proportion of the population wishing to engage in wilderness-based recreation activities will increase throughout the U.S."

[emphases added throughout]

3

PRESERVATION OF RAPTOR HABITAT ON THE SNAKE RIVER: A UNIQUE USE FOR ARID WILDLANDS

Carl D. Marti

INTRODUCTION

An unusual concentration of nesting raptors (owls, hawks, eagles, falcons, and vultures), possibly the world's densest, occurs along the Snake River in southwestern Idaho (Newton 1979, Kochert and Pellant 1986). This large aggregation of birds of prey is possible because of the coexistence of abundant nesting sites, plentiful prey resources, and a favorable climate. Much of this raptor habitat is public land managed by the U.S. Bureau of Land Management (BLM), and many competing users vie for it. Some of the highly varied applications (discussed below) are compatible with nesting raptors, but others are not and the birds will survive there only if humans practice good stewardship of the land.

These lands do not meet criteria for designation under the Wilderness Act; the imprint of humans exceeds the limits set in the Act. However, the Snake River Birds of Prey Area (SRBOPA) contains many of the characteristics of lands included in the National Wilderness Preservation System. In particular, the Snake River Canyon, the heart of this region, offers solitude and scenic vistas comparable to many designated or proposed wilderness areas. Indeed, the raptors themselves symbolize wildness and wildlands.

Humans have treated raptors in an equivocal manner, persecuting them severely on the one hand (Newton 1979), while on the other hand, many admire the finely honed adaptations of raptors for detecting and capturing prey. Today, increasing numbers of people value the chance to see raptors or to know simply that they exist somewhere.

In this chapter I describe the assemblage of birds of prey on the Snake River, detail the history of attempts to protect it, and discuss various uses for this public land. Finally, I discuss the alternatives of preserving or not preserving birds-of-prey nesting habitat on the Snake River.

THE RAPTOR ASSEMBLAGE AND ITS HABITAT

The SRBOPA lies about 48 km south of Boise, Idaho in Canyon, Ada, Elmore, and Owhyee counties between 770 and 1300 m in elevation. Its principal physiographic feature is the Snake River Canyon bounded by basalt cliffs ranging from 2 to 125 m in height. Plateau lands along the canyon are gently rolling and punctuated with isolated buttes. The native vegetation is characteristic of shrubsteppe communities, with big sagebrush (*Artemisia tridentata*), shadscale (*Atriplex confertifolia*), and winterfat (*Ceratoides lanata*) associations dominating. Many introduced plant species occur, including the very common cheatgrass (*Bromus tectorum*). About 19% of the area is under irrigation farming. Annual precipitation averages 20 cm and temperatures range from −0.5°C in January to 24.0°C in July. Comprehensive descriptions of the climate and vegetation of this area are in the United States Department of the Interior (1979).

Over seven hundred pairs of fifteen raptor species nest annually in the SRBOPA (Kochert and Pellant 1986; Table 3.1). An additional nine raptors use the area for wintering or in migration (Table 3.2). Several species of vertebrates that occur on the SRBOPA including six raptors are listed as endangered species by the U.S. Fish and Wildlife Service or sensitive species by the BLM and the Idaho Department of Fish and Game (Table 3.3).

HISTORY OF PROTECTION AND EVALUATION

Presently, the SRBOPA is a 240,064-ha preserve (193,056 ha of which is public land) along a 130-km stretch of the Snake River (Figure 3.1). The boundaries of the SRBOPA include some private and state-owned lands. These private and state-owned inholdings are not affected by any of the policies set for the BLM lands.

First protection for raptor habitat on the Snake River occurred in 1971 (Muhn and Stuart 1988). Secretary of the Interior Rodgers Morton withdrew a narrow 12,890 ha (10,685 ha public) site termed the Snake River Birds of Prey Natural Area (SRBPNA) along 53 km of the canyon. In 1972, the BLM initiated a comprehensive year-around study of the raptors, their prey, and the vegetation patterns. These investigations revealed that the original withdrawal protected only a small part of the important nesting areas and very little of the foraging habitat of several important raptors. Also revealed was that conversion of publicly owned arid lands to irrigated farmlands under two federal acts (the Desert Land Act passed in 1877, and the Carey Act, passed in 1894) resulted in significant loss of foraging habitat. Townsend ground squirrels (*Spermophilus townsendii*) and black-tailed jackrabbits (*Lepus californicus*), important foods of prairie falcons (*Falco mexicanus*), golden eagles (*Aquila*

Table 3.1   Number of pairs of raptors nesting in
the Snake River Birds of Prey Area
(BLM unpublished data)[1]

Species	Maximum number of territorial pairs/year
Turkey Vulture	
(*Cathartes aura*)	2
Northern Harrier	
(*Circus cyaneus*)	86
Swainson's Hawk	
(*Buteo swainsoni*)	3
Red-tailed Hawk	
(*B. jamaicensis*)	71
Ferruginous Hawk	
(*B. regalis*)	31
Golden Eagle	
(*Aquila chrysaetos*)	35
American Kestrel	
(*Falco sparverius*)	44
Prairie Falcon	
(*F. mexicanus*)	208
Barn Owl	
(*Tyto alba*)	69
Western Screech-owl	
(*Otus kennicottii*)	19
Great Horned Owl	
(*Bubo virginianus*)	44
Burrowing Owl	
(*Speotyto cunnicularia*)	24
Long-eared Owl	
(*Asio otus*)	64
Short-eared Owl	
(*A. flammeus*)	3
Northern Saw-whet Owl	
(*Aegolius acadicus*)	8

[1]Data are from 1973–1990. Not all species were completely
surveyed in every year. Numbers for each species represent
the maximum number of pairs counted in any given year.

Table 3.2   Winter visitor or migrant species in the
                        Snake River Birds of Prey Area

Osprey (*Pandion haliaetus*)
Bald Eagle (*Haliaeetus leucocephalus*)
Sharp-shinned Hawk (*Accipiter striatus*)
Cooper's Hawk (*A. cooperi*)
Northern Goshawk (*A. gentilis*)
Rough-legged Hawk (*Buteo lagopus*)
Merlin (*Falco columbarius*)
Peregrine Falcon (*F. peregrinus*)
Gyrfalcon (*F. rusticolus*)

chryseatos), and red-tailed hawks (*Buteo jamaicensis*) declined or disappeared when rangelands were converted to irrigated farms. In 1975, the Idaho State Director of the BLM used this information to set aside an additional 193,862 ha (121,976 ha public) of land adjacent to the SRBPNA called the Birds of Prey Study Area (BPSA). Because the BPSA contained habitat believed to be significant to the raptors and their prey, the BLM District Manager issued a temporary moratorium on claims filed under the Carey Act and the Desert Land Act. However, other actions potentially in conflict with preservation of raptor habitat—grazing and military training—were allowed to continue. By 1977 it was apparent that the raptors were using even more land for hunting than first realized, and the boundaries of the BPSA were expanded by another 139,344 ha (93,610 ha public). With these two expansions, 333,206 ha (215,586 ha public) along 104 km of the Snake River were temporarily protected.

Table 3.3.   Endangered and sensitive vertebrate species
                        occurring in the Snake River Birds of Prey Area.

Species	Status
White Sturgeon (*Acipenser transmontanus*)	sensitive
Western Ground Snake (*Sonora semiannulata*)	sensitive
Spotted Bat (*Euderma maculatum*)	sensitive
River Otter (*Lutra canadensis*)	sensitive
Bobcat (*Felis rufus*)	sensitive
Osprey (*Pandion haliaetus*)	sensitive
Bald Eagle (*Haliaeetus leucocephalus*)	endangered
Ferruginous Hawk (*Buteo regalis*)	sensitive
Merlin (*Falco columbarus*)	sensitive
Peregrine Falcon (*F. peregrinus*)	endangered
Long-billed Curlew (*Numenius americanus*)	sensitive
Burrowing Owl (*Speotyto cunnicularia*)	sensitive

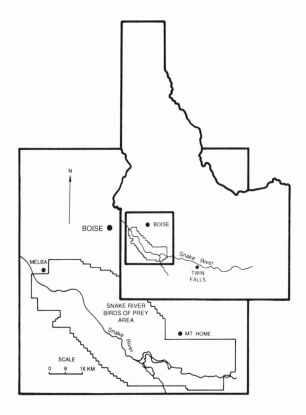

Figure 3.1. Location of the Snake River Birds of Prey Area.

In 1979 the BLM submitted a proposal to Congress for the creation of the Snake River Birds of Prey National Conservation Area (SRBPNCA). The boundaries of this proposed preserve were determined by first identifying the area that the raptor assemblage needed for nesting and foraging habitat. Land-ownership, land uses, and political boundaries were then considered to modify the biological boundaries, resulting in a proposal for protection of 240,064 ha. The SRBPNCA would have encompassed 193,056 ha of federally owned land, 15,872 ha of state land, and 31,136 ha of private land. Neither state nor private land within the boundaries would have been affected by the proposal. By 1980 Congress had not acted on the proposal, and it was apparent that no protection was likely with the Reagan administration on the horizon. Instead, Secretary of the Interior Cecil Andrus designated 193,056 ha of federal land as the Snake River Birds of Prey Area (SRBOPA) under section 204 of the Federal Land Policy and Management Act (FLPMA). This order withdrew the canyon from general mining and halted further agricultural development or other conversion to private ownership on plateau lands. The order is only for twenty years and can be modified, rescinded, or renewed at any time. Therefore, this unique, important Snake River raptor habitat still does not have permanent protection.

The BLM continues to conduct the research begun on the SRBPNA in 1972. Phase I of the research was conducted by BLM personnel and by university scientists under contract to the BLM. It focused on determining raptor densities and reproductive performances, feeding of the raptors and other predators, density and distribution of prey species, and patterns of vegetative cover. The BLM proposed to begin a second phase of research in 1981 to examine the relationships between raptors and their habitat and between prey species and their habitat, as well as the role of fire and livestock grazing on the SRBOPA. These projects were never funded. Instead, the BLM devoted its research efforts in the 1980s to monitoring population densities of selected raptor species and to analyzing and publishing data already collected. Starting in 1990, a five-year research project will investigate the effects of military training on the raptors, their prey, and their habitat. This project will also assess the effects of range fires and livestock grazing.

In 1982, the BLM outlined a management plan for the SRBOPA under the philosophy of allowing high levels of multiple use without threatening the existence of the raptors and their habitat (United States Department of the Interior 1985). Four goals were specified in the plan: (1) to perpetuate the nesting raptor populations at or above the minimum population levels determined for each species between 1975 and 1981; (2) to provide for other compatible uses in the Area; (3) to coordinate and conduct research and studies to support management needs; and (4) to make available to the public, other agencies, and the scientific community knowledge gained from management and research activities.

ALTERNATE LAND USES

Raptor Habitat

The high density of raptors in the SRBOPA affirms that the region is quality habitat for these birds. That this concentration of relatively rare birds is so unique in the entire world (Newton 1979) argues strongly for making preservation of raptor habitat the keystone for management of these lands. Such an ecosystem-scale preserve has multiple values. These include: (1) serving as a site for ecological studies; (2) providing opportunities for recreational wildlife observation; and (3) preservation of a portion of the national wilderness–historical–cultural heritage.

The abundance of scientific literature originating from research there attests that the SRBOPA is an excellent outdoor laboratory for ecological research. By the end of 1989, fifty-seven papers derived from SRBOPA studies had been published in professional journals. Most of these dealt directly with raptors (see, for example, Steenhof and Kochert 1982, 1985, 1988, Collopy 1983, Marks 1986, Marti 1988). Other subjects were mammalian and reptilian predators (see, for example, Messick and Hornocker 1981, Diller and Johnson 1988), prey species (see, for example, Smith et al. 1984, Smith and Johnson 1985, Johnson et al. 1987, Groves and Steenhof 1988), and vegetative composition and management (Hyde et al. 1982, Yensen 1982, Kochert and Pellant 1986). An additional nineteen papers from SRBOPA work appeared as technical reports or in symposium proceedings. A complete bibliography of SRBOPA publications is found in Steenhof (1989).

Bird watching is the second most popular passive sport in North America, with thirty million participants (Ehrlich et al. 1988). Birds of prey, because of their relative rarity and array of fascinating adaptations, are of particular interest to nature watchers. In the 1970s the BLM recorded over 1,000 visitor days per year for bird watching (United States Department of the Interior 1980). Visitor use of the SRBOPA has increased 13% per year since 1981; in 1985, 17,500 people used the core area between the town of Grandview and the Guffey railroad bridge (Shallat 1987). Bird watching was the activity of 9.3% of visitors who entered at one of the major access points from 1984 to 1987 (Holthuijzen 1989). This high visitation rate occurs despite the fact that the SRBOPA is remote, has few directional signs on highway approaches, and has only one interpretational facility (built in 1986). Visitation rates by bird watchers will undoubtedly increase when the area becomes better known.

The American public desires that wild places and wild animals exist somewhere even if they will never see them. A powerful example of this are donations by the public to the Nature Conservancy that enable the protection of 2,270,395 ha of land in fifty states (Anonymous 1990). Indeed, it is highly likely that most of the contributors to this and other conservation organizations have not been to the areas that their donations help to protect. Specifically in regard to the SRBOPA, the Nature Conservancy raised 300,000 dollars to purchase several critical inholdings of private land there.

Foreshadowing the modern environmental movement, Leopold (1949) made an eloquent plea for humans to treat the land and other species with the same ethics they practiced among themselves. When his essay "The Land Ethic" was written, regrettably little progress had been made in overturning the philosophy that humans had the right to conquer the land. The fifty-odd years following publication of that essay have seen some progress in human stewardship of the land. Unfortunately, a significant number of people today retain the nature-is-there-to-serve-man philosophy. Leopold said, "Quit thinking about decent land-use as solely an economic problem. . . . A thing is right when it tends to preserve the integrity, stability, and beauty of the biotic community. It is wrong when it tends otherwise." Under this philosophy, preserving the Snake River Birds of Prey Area is ethically right.

Cultural Resources

Evidence of human occupancy on the SRBOPA spans fifteen thousand years. This area is believed to have been one of the most densely occupied regions in southwestern Idaho during prehistoric times (Swanson 1965), harboring over two hundred archeological sites (United States Department of the Interior 1990). These sites are notable not only in number, but also in size, lack of disturbance, and variety. The Black Butte/Guffey Butte Archeological District, which conforms with the boundaries of the original SRBPNA, is on the National Register of Historic Places. Several other archeological sites in the SRBOPA are under consideration for listing on the Register.

Relics of historical times include portions of the Oregon Trail (part of the National Trails System) and associated campsites and emigrant graves. The Guffey Railroad Bridge and townsite, relics of gold and silver mining activities, are also on the National Register of Historic Places. Many other sites of historic value representing early days of emigration, mining, ranching, and railroading also occur within the SRBOPA (Shallat 1987).

The SRBOPA is also known to be an area of high significance in paleontological research (Schultz 1937, Shotwell 1970, Conrad 1980). At least twelve fossil-rich sites have been reported. These sites have yielded a wide variety of fossils including plants, fish, mollusks, and large mammals. A large, continuous layer of potentially fossil-bearing deposits in the SRBOPA has not yet been adequately inventoried, but it suggests the possibility of additional fossil sites.

Recreation

Fishing heads a wide range of outdoor recreation activities occurring on the SRBOPA; a recent survey found that fishing was the intended activity of 36.6% of the visitors (Holthuijzen 1989). Other water-associated recreation includes waterfowl hunting and river running. Camping, picnicking, and sight-seeing are also popular activities. Visitors come to the SRBOPA to see both geological features and wildlife. Off-road vehicular recreation is popular in the vicinity. However, the BLM has imposed a year-around prohibition against driving motorized vehicles off designated roads in the SRBOPA. Another closure designed to protect the nesting raptors is a prohibition against shooting from March to August. Unfortunately, the shooting closure applies only to the area of the original SRBPNA and not the entire SRPOBA.

Minerals

The area encompassing the SRBOPA has had little historical mineral-extraction activity. Several permits are presently in effect for removal of sand, gravel, and volcanic cinders, and two small claims for clay removal are also active (United States Department of the Interior 1980). Although placer gold mining has occurred on the Snake River, no operations currently exist within the SRBOPA. Of leasable minerals, only oil, gas, and geothermal are believed to occur in the area. Eighty-four oil and gas leases covering 57,970 ha and seventeen geothermal leases covering 10,350 ha are active in the SRBOPA in 1980 (United States Department of the Interior 1980). The small amount of prospecting done and the absence of any active mineral wells seem to indicate that the SRBOPA has little mineral potential in the present market. Further mineral claims have been prohibited in an area of the SRBOPA extending 0.4 km from the canyon (Kochert and Pellant 1986).

Military Training

Since 1953 the Idaho National Guard has conducted military training exercises within the present SRBOPA. Most activity occurs in June, July, and August and involves tank maneuvering, artillery firing, and bivouacking troops. The boundary and size of this area have been adjusted several times. In 1973 the BLM concluded that the boundary should be moved back at least 3.2 km from the canyon rim to protect nesting raptors and reduce soil erosion. After the passage of FLPMA, National Guard use has been authorized by a Memorandum of Understanding between the BLM and the Guard that is reviewed every five years. The Guard now uses 52,400 ha of land called the Orchard Training Area (about one-third of the area of the SRBOPA).

Agriculture

Farming. Fertile soils along the Snake River have much potential for farming pending the availability of water. Essentially, all farming there requires irrigation and water is a significant limiting factor. About 68% of the private land within the SRBOPA is farmed for potatoes, sugar beets, beans, corn, grain, and alfalfa. In 1974, 289 applications were on file with the BLM for transfer of an additional 52,000 ha of public land to private ownership for farming development. These claims, filed under the Carey Act and the Desert Land Act, were put on hold in 1974 and subsequently denied (Kochert and Pellant 1986). Furthermore, water necessary to develop these claims is difficult to obtain. A moratorium on applications for new water development was in effect through most of the 1980s. Though the moratorium is now lifted, obtaining new water rights is subject to serious delays because of a backlog of applications and continuing controversy over future water supplies (Steve Lester, personal communication).

Grazing. Livestock grazing has been the dominant agricultural activity within the SRBOPA since 1870 (Yensen 1982). Grazing in the SRBOPA is mainly by cattle in spring, fall, and winter. A total of 46,000 animal unit months (AUMs) are divided among sixty-six permittees. Only three permittees graze sheep on the SRBOPA, totaling 14,600 AUMs (United States Department of the Interior 1980).

Most land currently managed by the BLM had been seriously degraded by heavy overgrazing of livestock before it came under BLM control (Barton 1987). In southwestern Idaho, the effects of early overgrazing were compounded by severe drought and the introduction of exotic plants, particularly cheatgrass. Together, these resulted in nearly complete elimination of native grasses by the 1930s (Yensen 1982). Secondary successional patterns have also been altered because of these conditions. Instead of the reestablishment of big sagebrush following disturbance, continuous stands of cheatgrass occurred by 1949 (Stewart and Hull 1949). Many acres of BLM lands were planted with crested wheatgrass (*Agropyron* spp.) primarily to improve ranges for livestock grazing (Young and Evans 1986). These wheatgrass monocultures are poor wildlife habitat, but they can be diversified by planting shrubs (McKell 1986).

Which Alternatives Are Best and Mutually Compatible?

If preservation of raptor habitat is accepted as the driving force for managing these lands along the Snake River, what other land uses are compatible? Preserving and studying paleontological and prehistoric and historic human sites would cause no conflicts for raptors. Indeed, protection of raptor habitat would help protect these valuable cultural sites from vandalism, illegal collecting, and destruction through farmland conversion.

The impacts of recreation are more diverse. Some are potentially damaging to raptors and must be regulated, but many can continue in harmony with the raptor populations. Recreational activities certainly have the potential to affect nesting raptors adversely (Knight and Skagen 1988). Any human activity that causes raptors to flush from their nests and stay away for extended periods can reduce reproductive success. Unfortunately, few data are available to document these effects (Knight and Skagen 1988). One study concluded that only 2.4% of the human visitors to the SRBOPA were involved in activities potentially disturbing to raptors, and in general, recreational activities had no detectable adverse effects on nesting prairie falcons there (Holthuijzen 1989).

Permanent establishment of a bird of prey conservation area undoubtedly would attract even more visitors, and it will require added educational and control efforts by the BLM. Noise and damage to vegetation and soil are problems created by off-road vehicle recreation; they can be minimized by continuing the prohibition against driving vehicles off designated roads and, if necessary, by closing critical nesting areas. Other, minor activities such as rock climbing can be mitigated by education and the closing of critical areas to climbing during the nesting season. The prohibition against recreational shooting during the nesting season must be expanded to cover the entire SRBOPA. Hunting and fishing are popular recreational activities that seem to have little adverse effect on the raptors. In the case of fishing, activity is usually not close to the nesting habitat. Hunting occurs in fall and winter when no nesting is occurring and when raptor populations are lowest on the SRBOPA.

In 1979, the BLM concluded that twenty-five years of military training had had no known effect on the raptors. However, no studies had specifically addressed the questions of conflicts between the training and raptor habitat preservation. Research designed to assess potential effects began in 1990, spurred by proposed upgrades of the Orchard Training Area: relocation of tank and ammunition storage adjacent to the training area and upgrading of the tank range to state-of-the-art technology.

Further expansion of farming appears to be incompatible with preserving the Snake River raptor habitat. Newton (1986) and De Molenaar (1983) identified agriculture as a major reason for declines of raptors in intensively farmed Europe. Young (1989) provides a comprehensive review of the effects (many of them adverse) of agriculture on raptors in the western United States.

Both farming and grazing may adversely affect raptor populations. However, grazing is generally considered to be more compatible with raptor preservation on the SRBOPA than is farming. Hyde et al. (1982) asserted that the choice between preserving raptor habitat and developing farmland could be made by comparing the economic benefits of grazing and farming. If the benefits of grazing exceed the benefits of farming, then raptor habitat preservation is more economically justifiable. Under the assumption that grazing and raptor habitat preservation are compatible, the nonmarket values of preserving raptors (for example, aesthetics and as environmental monitors) need not be considered in the decision. Hyde et al. (1982) concluded that benefits of grazing exceeded those of farming in the long term and probably in the short term. Availability of water and the cost of electricity to distribute it for irrigation are major limiting factors for farming.

Many interacting variables cloud the effects of grazing on raptors and other wildlife (Kochert et al. 1988). In general, grazing is viewed as a major threat to wildlife habitat (Barton 1987). In some cases grazing may be directly detrimental to ground nesting raptors (Duebbert and Lokemoen 1977). However, grazing may also produce vegetative conditions favorable to some important raptor prey (Taylor et al. 1935, Flinders and Hansen 1975). The effects of livestock grazing on the SRBOPA have not been fully evaluated, and it is apparent that continuous monitoring must occur.

Impacts of Preservation

Public lands historically have been managed for multiple uses. Sometimes this approach is successful. In other cases, the incompatibility of some applications restricts uses of the land. Management agencies acting on the desires of the public must often make decisions that will favor certain uses at the expense of others. In the case of the SRBOPA it is reasonably clear which land uses are desired by the public and which are mutually compatible (United States Department of the Interior 1980). The following summarizes the major outcomes of preserving or not preserving raptor habitat on the Snake River.

Positive. Permanently withdrawing land proposed to form the SRBPNCA would provide total ecosystem protection; that is, the birds, their nest sites, and their prey base would be protected. It would do much to ensure the survival of an assemblage of birds with great biological and aesthetic value. This method of preservation would also retain multiple use of public lands. Archeological and paleontological study and preservation, some livestock grazing, and many forms of recreation would be likely to continue.

Negative. Establishment of the SRBPNCA would prevent the development of additional irrigated farmlands there. It would also prohibit some future mineral exploration and attract larger numbers of visitors, potentially increasing impacts on the land. Compared to the positive values, these negative aspects are minor. The economic benefits of farming there have been shown to be less than those of its alternative—grazing—an activity that would probably continue. Mineral extraction appears to have limited potential, so its prohibition would seem to be unimportant. The effects of increasing numbers of visitors could be mitigated by additional educational and enforcement efforts by the BLM and associated organizations.

CONCLUSION

The lands currently known as the Snake River Birds of Prey Area are used for many purposes. Designating these public lands to serve primarily as raptor habitat would recognize the area's most unique feature. Such a designation also has some economic support in terms of livestock grazing and recreational pursuits. Preservation of raptor habitat is compatible with a number of human uses but not with others. Those incompatible uses should be eliminated and certain other uses whose effects are not well known should be carefully monitored.

ACKNOWLEDGMENTS

I thank Karen Steenhof, Analytical Research Biologist, Birds of Prey Research, BLM, and Mike Kochert, Associate Leader, Birds of Prey Research, BLM, for supplying many documents and much information on the Snake River Birds of Prey Area. Margaret Wyatt, Archaeologist, BLM, graciously provided information on cultural resources of the area, and Ted Weasma, Paleontologist, BLM, provided key references regarding the paleontological knowledge of the Snake River plain. Steve Lester, Senior Water Resource Agent, Idaho Department of Water Resources, gave me insights on the complicated problems of water rights in southwestern Idaho. I also thank Cyrus McKell, Karen Steenhof, and Samuel Zeveloff for critical reviews of this chapter.

REFERENCES

Anonymous. 1990. *Nature Conservancy Magazine* 40:2.

Barton, K. 1987. "Bureau of Land Management." In R. L. Di Silvestro (ed.) *Audubon Wildlife Report 1987*. Orlando, Fla.: Academic Press, pp. 3–59.

Collopy, M. W. 1983. "Foraging Behavior and Success of Golden Eagles." *Auk* 100:747–749.

Conrad, G. S. 1980. "The Biostratigraphy and Mammalian Paleontology of the Glen's Ferry Formation from Hammett to Oreana, Idaho" Ph.D. Dissertation. Pocatello, Idaho: Idaho State University.

De Molenaar, J. G. 1983. "Agriculture and Its Effects on Birdlife in Europe." In P. Goriup (ed.) *Agriculture and Birdlife in Europe*. Cambridge, England: International Council for Bird Preservation, pp. 13–34.

Diller, L. V., and D. R. Johnson. 1988. "Food Habits, Consumption Rates, and Predation Rates of Western Rattlesnakes and Gopher Snakes in Southwestern Idaho." *Herpetologica* 44:228–233.

Duebbert, H. F., and J. T. Lokemoen. 1977. "Upland Nesting of American Bitterns, Marsh Hawks, and Short-eared Owls." *Prairie Naturalist* 9:33–40.

Ehrlich, P. R., D. S. Dobkin, and D. Wheye. 1988. *The Birder's Handbook*. New York: Simon and Schuster.

Flinders, J. T., and R. M. Hansen. 1975. "Spring Population Responses of Cottontails and Black-Tailed Jackrabbits to Cattle Grazing Short Grass Prairie." *Journal of Range Management* 28:290–293.

Groves, C. R., and K. Steenhof. 1988. "Responses of Small Mammals and Vegetation to Wildfire in Shadscale Communities of Southwestern Idaho." *Northwest Science* 62:205–210.

Holthuijzen, A. M. A. 1989. *Behavior and Productivity of Nesting Prairie Falcons in Relation to Construction Activities at Swan Falls Dam*. Boise, Idaho: Idaho Power Company.

Hyde, W. F., A. Dickerman, and D. Stone. 1982. "Development versus Preservation in the Snake River Birds of Prey Conservation Area." *American Journal of Agricultural Economics* 64:756–760.

Johnson, D. R., N. C. Nydegger, and G. W. Smith. 1987. "Comparison of Movement-based Density Estimates for Townsend Ground Squirrels." *Journal of Mammalogy* 68:689–691.

Knight, R. L., and S. K. Skagen. 1988. "Effects of Recreational Disturbance on Birds of Prey: A Review." In R. L. Glinski, B. G. Pendleton, M. B. Moss, M. N. LeFranc, and S. W. Hoffman (eds.) *Proceedings of the Southwest Raptor Management Symposium and Workshop.* Washington, D.C.: National Wildlife Federation Science and Technical Series No. 11, pp. 355–359.

Kochert, M. N., B. A. Millsap, and K. Steenhof. 1988. "Effects of Livestock Grazing on Raptors with Emphasis on the Southwestern U.S." In R. L. Glinski, B. G. Pendleton, M. B. Moss, M. N. LeFranc, and S. W. Hoffman, (eds.) *Proceedings of the Southwest Raptor Management Symposium and Workshop.* Washington, D.C.: National Wildlife Federation Science and Technical Series No. 11, pp. 325–334.

Kochert, M. N., and M. Pellant. 1986. "Multiple Use in the Snake River Birds of Prey Area." *Rangelands* 8:217–220.

Leopold, A. 1949. *A Sand County Almanac and Sketches Here and There.* New York: Oxford University Press.

Marks, J. S. 1986. "Nest-site Characteristics and Reproductive Success of Long-eared Owls in Southwestern Idaho." *Wilson Bulletin* 98:547–560.

Marks, J. S., J. H. Doremus, and R. J. Cannings. 1989. "Polygyny in the Northern Saw-whet Owl." *Auk* 106:732–734.

Marti, C. D. 1988. "A Long-term Study of Food-niche Dynamics in the Common Barn-Owl: Comparisons within and between Populations." *Canadian Journal of Zoology* 66:1803–1812.

McKell, C. M. 1986. "The Role of Shrubs in Diversifying a Crested Wheatgrass Monoculture." In K. L. Johnson (ed.) *Crested Wheatgrass: Its Values, Problems, and Myths; Symposium Proceedings.* Logan, Utah: Utah State University, pp. 109–115.

Messick, J. P., and M. G. Hornocker. 1981. *Ecology of the Badger in Southwestern Idaho.* Wildlife Monographs 76.

Muhn, J., and H. R. Stuart. 1988. *Opportunity and Challenge, the Story of BLM.* Washington, D.C.: United States Department of the Interior, Bureau of Land Management.

Newton, I. 1979. *Population Ecology of Raptors.* Vermillion, S.D.: Buteo Books.

———. 1986. "Future Prospects for Raptors in Europe." *Raptor Research Report* 5:4–10.

Schultz, J. 1937. "Late Cenozoic Vertebrate Fauna from the Coso Mountains, Inyo County, California." In R. W. Wilson (ed.) *Studies on Cenozoic Vertebrates of Western North America.* Contributions to Paleontology no. 3. Washington, D.C.: Carnegie Institution of Washington.

Shallat, T. (ed.) 1987. *Prospects, Land-use in the Snake River Birds of Prey Area.* Social Science Monographs no. 1. Boise, Idaho: Boise State University.

Shotwell, J. A. 1970. *Pleiocene Mammals of Southeastern Oregon and Adjacent Idaho.* Museum of Natural History Bulletin no. 17. Eugene: University of Oregon.

Smith, G. W., and D. R. Johnson. 1985. "Demography of a Townsend Ground Squirrel Population in Southwestern Idaho." *Ecology* 66:171–178.

Smith, G. W., N. C. Nydegger, and D. L. Yensen. 1984. "Passerine Bird Densities in Shrubsteppe Vegetation." *Journal of Field Ornithology* 55:261–264.

Steenhof, K. (ed.) 1989. *Snake River Birds of Prey, 1989 Annual Report.* Boise, Idaho: United States Department of the Interior, Bureau of Land Management.

Steenhof, K., and M. N. Kochert. 1982. "An Evaluation of Methods used to Estimate Raptor Nesting Success." *Journal of Wildlife Management* 46:885–893.

Steenhof, K., and M. N. Kochert. 1985. "Dietary Shifts of Sympatric Buteos during a Prey Decline." *Oecologia* 66:6–16.

Steenhof, K., and M. N. Kochert. 1988. "Dietary Responses of Three Raptor Species to Changing Prey Densities in a Natural Environment." *Journal of Animal Ecology* 57:37–48.

Stewart, G., and A. C. Hull. 1949. "Cheatgrass in Southern Idaho." *Ecology* 30:58–74.

Swanson, E. H. 1965. "Archaeological Explorations in Southwestern Idaho." *American Antiquity* 31:24–37.

Taylor, W. P., C. T. Vorhies, and P. B. Lister. 1935. "The Relation of Jackrabbits to Grazing in Southern Arizona." *Journal of Forestry* 33:490–498.

United States Department of the Interior. 1979. *Snake River Birds of Prey, Special Research Report.* Boise, Idaho: United States Department of the Interior, Bureau of Land Management.

———. 1980. *Final Environmental Statement, Snake River Birds of Prey Conservation Area.* Boise, Idaho: United States Department of the Interior, Bureau of Land Management.

———. 1985. *Snake River Birds of Prey Area Management Plan.* Boise, Idaho: United States Department of the Interior, Bureau of Land Management.

Yensen, D. 1982. *A Grazing History of Southwestern Idaho with Emphasis on the Birds of Prey Study Area.* Boise, Idaho: United States Department of the Interior, Bureau of Land Management.

Young, J. A., and R. A. Evans. 1986. "History of Crested Wheatgrass in the Intermountain Area." In K. L. Johnson (ed.) *Crested Wheatgrass: Its Values, Problems, and Myths; Symposium Proceedings.* Logan, Utah: Utah State University, pp. 21–25.

Young, L. S. 1989. "Effects of Agriculture on Raptors in the Western United States: An Overview." In B. G. Pendleton (ed.) *Proceedings of the Western Raptor Managment Symposium and Workshop.* Washington, D.C.: National Wildlife Federation, Science and Technical Series no. 12, pp. 209–218.

4

BIGHORN SHEEP AND HORSES ON THE BIGHORN CANYON NATIONAL RECREATION AREA: WILDERNESS OR PASTURE?

Mark S. Boyce, Lee H. Metzgar, and J. Terry Peters

INTRODUCTION

Federal agencies managing western wildlands usually have clear policy that native species are given management preference over exotics. Indeed, exotics are usually classified as weedy species to be controlled or eliminated whenever possible. However, feral horses (*Equus cabalus*) present a contradiction because of popular sentiment favoring the maintenance of horses on our public lands.

Feral horses inhabit vast areas of arid lands in the western United States, where they have the potential to compete with a diversity of domestic and wild ungulates. Horses on public lands were protected from mustanging and other inhumane treatment by the Wild Horse and Burro Act of 1971 (Public Law 92-195, S. 1116, 85 Stat. 649), and horses rapidly became so numerous that, in a number of areas, they had reputedly caused range degradation and had become serious competitors with domestic livestock and wildlife. Consequently, all populations of feral horses on public lands are controlled, mostly through roundups, with horses being offered in the U.S. Bureau of Land Management's (BLM's) "adopt a horse" program.

A conflict with feral horse management is developing in north-central Wyoming and south-central Montana because bighorn sheep (*Ovis canadensis*) are recolonizing formerly used areas on the Bighorn Canyon National Recreation Area (BICA) and the Pryor Mountain Wild Horse Range (PMWHR). Competition between horses and bighorns may require that populations of either or both species be reduced. Although the National Park Service has officially designated portions of the BICA for use by feral horses, agency policy favors priority management for native taxa (Dennis 1980).

In this chapter we review the ecology and management of feral horses and bighorn sheep on the BICA and the PMWHR, and present information on competition between these species that could be relevant to the management of these species in wilderness areas. We develop a model of competition between horses and bighorns, and use this model to make predictions of the probable future dynamics of the system under various management alternatives. Finally, we discuss management implications in the context of Park Service policy regarding the management of exotic species.

STUDY AREA

The Bighorn Canyon National Recreation Area was established by congressional order in 1966 (80 Stat. 913; 16 U.S.C. 460t) and is managed by the National Park Service of the U.S. Department of Interior (Figure 4.1). The 48,583-ha area encompasses a 113-km-long reservoir created by the construction of the Yellowtail Dam, dedicated in 1968.

Immediately adjacent to the BICA on the Wyoming–Montana border is the Pryor Mountain Wild Horse Range, which was one of the first areas in the United States to be officially recognized for its feral horse population (Fed. Reg. 33[178], 12 September 1968). The PMWHR encompasses approximately 13,000 ha, with the horse herd managed by the BLM, which is also an agency of the U.S. Department of Interior. The legislation that established the PMWHR states that it "shall be in all respects subordinate to the Bighorn Canyon National Recreation Area established by the Act of October 15, 1966 (80 Stat. 913; 16 U.S.C. 460t), so far as it affects lands comprising any part of the Bighorn Canyon National Recreation Area."

In addition to BLM lands, 3,326 ha of the BICA have been designated wild horse range by a cooperative agreement between the National Park Service and the BLM. In addition, a 1,076-ha portion of the BICA, known as the Sorenson Extension, has been used for wild horse range on a special use permit from the National Park Service, but this permit was canceled in December 1989, and horses were removed on 29 June 1990. The U.S. Department of Agriculture Forest Service also permits horses from the PMWHR to graze on 1,538 ha of Custer National Forest that borders the PMWHR on the northwest.

Vegetation on the BICA has been mapped and characterized in detail by Knight et al. (1987). Aerial coverage of dominant vegetation communities are 40% juniper (*Juniperus osteosperma*)/curlleaf mountain mahogany (*Cercocarpus ledifolius*) woodland, 16% riparian vegetation, 15% desert shrubland, 12% sagebrush (*Artemisia* spp.) steppe, 8% grassland, and 6% coniferous woodland.

Horses were introduced to North America by the Spanish in the sixteenth century. The earliest records of horses in the BICA area are from circa 1900. Current management by the BLM maintains the horse herd at 121 animals.

Bighorn sheep were extirpated from the BICA, probably during the nine-

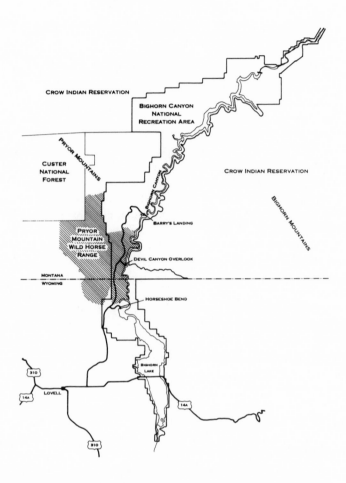

Figure 4.1. Map of the Bighorn Canyon National Recreation Area and the Pryor Mountain Wild Horse Range. Note that portions of the Horse Range overlap with the Bighorn Canyon National Recreation Area.

teenth century. In general, bighorn sheep populations have been declining throughout the western United States, but were reintroduced into the Bighorn Mountains east of the BICA during the mid-1970s (Coates and Schemnitz 1989). A few of these sheep eventually crossed the reservoir while it was ice-covered during winter and established a population on the west side of Bighorn Canyon. As of 1989, Bighorn Canyon hosted a population of approximately ninety-nine bighorns.

MINIMUM VIABLE POPULATION SIZE FOR BIGHORNS

A management program for bighorns and horses on the Bighorn Canyon National Recreation Area must aim for a density of sheep that will ensure the long-term survival of the population. During the past several decades, game management agencies in the western United States have made numerous attempts to restore bighorns in appropriate terrain where the species had been extirpated. Without exception, such attempts at recovery have been unsuccessful if the range supported fewer than 50 native animals (Berger 1990). The reason for this is not known with certainty, but it is known that inbred lines of bighorns suffer greater juvenile mortality (Sausman 1984).

The rule of thumb for minimum viable populations established by live-stock breeders is that one should maintain an effective population size of at least $N_e = 50$. For $N_e < 50$, inbreeding coefficients will increase by more than 1% per generation (Soule 1980). For bighorns, the total population necessary to achieve an effective population size of 50 should be substantially greater than 50 animals because fewer males than females have an opportunity to breed.

The effective population size is the number of animals that a population would contain if individuals of the opposite sex bred randomly with each other. Since only adult male bighorns breed, and males are less abundant than females, effective population size is bound to be smaller than the actual population size. Effective population size may be estimated by solving for N_e in the equation

$$1/N_e = 1/(4N_m) + 1/(4N_f) \tag{1}$$

where N_m and N_f are the number of breeding males and females, respectively, assuming nonoverlapping generations (Wright 1931). For the bighorn population at Bighorn Canyon, we used equation 1 to estimate an effective population of 44 for a total population of 99, 17 breeding males, and 32 breeding females. This is almost certainly a high estimate because we assumed that all males age 5 and older were reproductive. At this same adult sex ratio (17/32), at least 114 bighorn sheep will be necessary to produce an effective population of 50.

Hunting can reduce effective population size in bighorn sheep when it selectively removes mature breeding rams. Consequently, since the BICA population of bighorns is to be hunted, the population should be maintained at an even higher level. It is unknown whether the range will support 114 sheep and 121 horses for the long term, although range condition presumably is deteriorating under current stocking levels (Hall 1972, Coates and Schemnitz 1989).

Another concern regarding hunting this herd is that young, inexperienced rams may not know the location of prime seasonal ranges (Geist 1971). Therefore, hunting mature rams can upset the social system and require an even larger total population to ensure against environmental variance. Likewise, disturbance created by hunting can preclude sheep from using portions of their range and effectively reduce the carrying capacity of the habitat (Geist 1971).

COMPETITION BETWEEN HORSES AND BIGHORNS

Several studies have implicated feral equids as competitors with bighorn sheep (National Research Council 1982, Berger 1986). Horses typically dominate in social encounters with wildlife or livestock, for example, at water sources (Berger 1986, pp. 254–256). Horses have been observed to supplant bighorns in the Great Basin (Berger 1986), but behavioral dominance by horses over bighorns has not been demonstrated adequately. While diet overlap is substantial, Geist (1971) notes that "mountain sheep are some of the most specialized grazers, for they can live on hard, abrasive, dry plants."

Diet overlap of 0.78 between horses and bighorn sheep on the BICA (Coates and Schemnitz 1989) is similar to that occurring between horses and cattle in Colorado (Hansen and Clark 1977). Forage overlap varies seasonally, being highest during the summer when both species make heavy use of grasses, particularly bluebunch wheatgrass, *Agropyron spicatum* (Coates and Schemnitz 1989). During winter, sheep tend to use browse more than do horses.

However, competition between the two species is alleviated spatially because bighorn sheep can use terrain that is too steep for horses (Berger 1977, Ganskopp and Vavra 1987). Therefore, canyon areas of BICA afford a refuge for bighorn sheep where there is no competition for forage with horses.

Curiously, on the BICA, rams frequently forage with feral horses; ewes and lambs do so only occasionally. Alert behaviors are less frequent while foraging with horses than when they are with other bighorn sheep (Coates et al. 1988). Mixed-species group foraging is probably a predator-avoidance adaptation (Hamilton 1971).

Interspecific interactions between bighorn sheep and domestic sheep can lead to problems because the latter frequently transmits diseases and parasites to bighorns. This does not appear to be a great problem for horses and bighorns, although these two species share some parasites and diseases. Scabies mites can result in alopacia (hair loss) and thermoregulatory problems, and Lange et al. (1980) identified the same species of mite carried by horses on bighorn sheep, although their identification may have been in error because these mites are usually highly species-specific. Another parasite common to both species is *Setaria*, which causes cerebro-spinal nematodiasis (Beckland and Walker 1969). Although this nematode may be found in both bighorns and horses, it does not appear to cause symptoms in sheep frequently.

A MODEL OF COMPETITION UNDER EXPLOITATION

Traditional approaches to modeling competitive interaction, such as the Lotka-Volterra model, are not appropriate here because both species are exploited. It has long been recognized that predation or exploitation by man can alleviate competition and permit coexistence in otherwise unstable systems (Gausse 1935, Paine 1966). We have adapted an analytical model of competition under exploitation (Metzgar and Boyd 1989; Yodzis 1976, 1989; Derrick and Metzgar 1991) for the BICA sheep–horse interaction. Simulation modeling affords a viable alternative approach for gaining an understanding of the consequences of management alternatives for introduced populations (Hobbs et al. 1990).

We will build upon simultaneous differential equations of Lotka (1925) and Volterra (1926) for competition between horses, H, and bighorn sheep, B:

$$dB/dt \cdot 1/B = B'/B = r_B - cB - aH \tag{2}$$

$$H'/H = r_H - dH - fB \tag{3}$$

where the prime indicates the first derivative with respect to time; r_B and r_H are the potential per capita growth rates for bighorns and horses, respectively, in the absence of competition; c and d are intraspecific competition coefficients; and a and f are interspecific competition coefficients. We shall define the carrying capacity for bighorns to be $K_B = r_B/c$, and for horses $K_H = r_H/d$. This model yields four potential outcomes of competition depending upon the magnitude of carrying capacities and competition coefficients for each species. These include competitive exclusion of one or the other species, coexistence, or "contingency" where the initially most abundant species wins (Hutchinson 1965).

To incorporate exploitation, we employ a yield model which is an extension of the logistic model. Thus for horses we have:

$$H' = r_H H[1 - (H/K_H)^O] - C_H \tag{4}$$

where the O exponent determines the skew in the yield curve, and C_H is the annual cull of horses. This model may be illustrated graphically, as in Figure 4.2 with a new equilibrium population size, K_{cc}, existing where the C_H line intersects with the H'(H) curve to the right of the hump. The intersection to the left of the peak in the H'(H) curve is an unstable saddle point. A model of similar form may be developed for bighorn sheep.

Another way to illustrate the effect of exploitation is to plot the cull as a function of population size as shown in Figure 4.3. Here the yield curve is the combination of cull and population size that yield H' = 0, and the justifi-

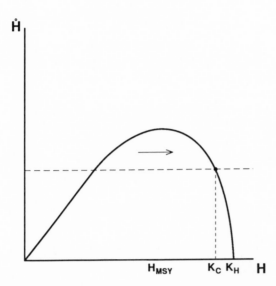

Figure 4.2. The rate of change in a horse population, H', as a function of horse population size, H. A cull of C horses is represented by the dashed horizontal line, yielding a new equilibrium population size, K_c. The maximum sustained yield of horses would occur for a population maintained as H_{MSY}.

cation for the shape of the curve is the same as Rosenzweig (1969) articulated for the prey curve in predator–prey models. Briefly, the yield curve intersects the abscissa to the right of the origin because of an Allee effect; that is, populations may actually decline for very small populations, for instance, due to inbreeding depression. The curve increases with increasing H because a larger population is able to sustain a larger cull, and the curve drops off to the right due to density dependence.

The magnitude of yield varies as a function of resource abundance, with the entire curve being elevated by enrichment. This is illustrated by the three-dimensional graph at Figure 4.4. For any cull rate, there is a combination of points where $H' = 0$, which form a curve convex to the H axis. This would entail taking a horizontal slice through the curved surface in Figure 4.4.

The same principle applies under competition for resources. As the abundance of a competitor increases, resources decrease resulting in a three-dimensional yield curve (Figure 4.5), which is essentially an inverse of the enrichment curve. Again, for a particular cull there is a static curve extracted as a horizontal slice from the three-dimensional surface. Such isoclines for three levels of horse cull are plotted in Figure 4.6.

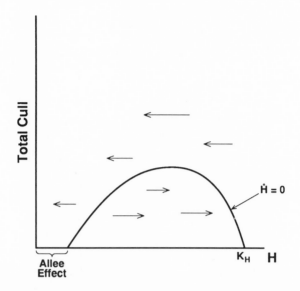

Figure 4.3. A yield curve for a horse population where the cull is
plotted against the horse population size, H. The curve is the combination of cull and population size at which there will be no change
in the horse population, that is, H' = 0. Underneath the curve,
the horse population will increase, whereas above it the population will decrease.

Figures 4.4, 4.5 and 4.6 are static plots for horses only. Similar relationships exist for bighorns as well, except that bighorns enjoy a refugium where
they can escape competition from horses. This refuge alters the shape of the
B' = 0 curve to something like that plotted in Figure 4.7. Indeed, if steep
terrain affords a "perfect" refugium, there could be theoretically an infinite
number of horses with no consequences to bighorn sheep at this range of
population sizes.

The outcome of competitive interaction between sheep and horses can be
determined by the intersection between the static curves for each species.
As in the simple Lotka-Volterra competition models, we may see coexistence
or competitive exclusion of either species, but here depending upon the cull.

In Figure 4.8, we have illustrated a circumstance that would yield stable
coexistence between horses and bighorn sheep, given continued culling of
horses. Note that the two curves intersect at three other points as well, but
each of these are unstable saddle points. Eventually, we expect to sustain an
equilibrium at the upper-right intersection between the two static curves.
Increasing the cull on horses causes a reduction in the equilibrium horse pop-

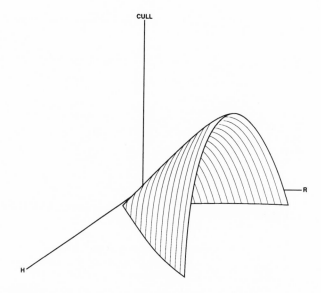

Figure 4.4. Yield curves as a function of the availability of some resource, R, such as food. The general shape of the yield curve is presumed to remain constant, but the carrying capacity and the maximum of the yield curve increase with increasing resources.

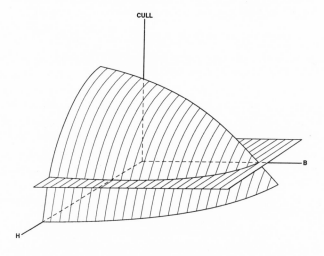

Figure 4.5. In contrast to Figure 4.4, yield curves decrease as a competitor, such as bighorn sheep, B, becomes more abundant. Imposing a constant cull irrespective of H or B is equivalent to slicing the cone-shaped set of yield curves with a plane.

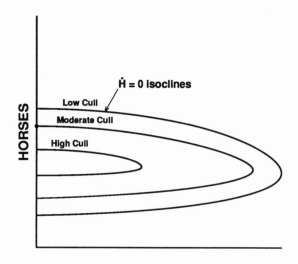

BIGHORNS

Figure 4.6. Another way of depicting Figure 4.5 is with isoclines of static curves, that is, where H' = 0, for low, moderate, and high cull rates. Currently, the feral horse population at the PMWHR is being sustained with a moderate cull, achieving approximate equilibrium at 121 horses. This point is depicted by a dot where the ordinate axis intersects the upper end of the moderate cull curve.

ulation and a concomitant increase in the bighorn population, as illustrated in Figure 4.9. If the peak in the horse curve should fall to the left of the right-hand slope of the sheep curve, we would observe a precipitous collapse in the horse population, followed by the sheep achieving carrying capacity.

On the other hand, culling of sheep runs the risk of a collapse in the sheep population and domination by horses (Figure 4.10). Again, this would depend upon the extent of the refugium for bighorns. If the habitat uniquely available to bighorns is inadequate to support a viable population, the sheep herd may decline to extinction.

For our calculations, ecological carrying capacity (see Caughley 1979) for horses is assumed to be approximately $K_H = 270$. Hall (1972) claims to have determined the carrying capacity of the PMWHR to be 85 horses, but no methods were presented. It appears that his calculations must have been to estimate the economic carrying capacity (Caughley 1979). The potential growth rate has been observed to be 20%, equivalent to a per capita growth rate of $r_H = 0.182$ (Garrott and Taylor 1990). The Pryor horses are relatively small in body size with females usually 270–340 kg and males 350–400 kg, accord-

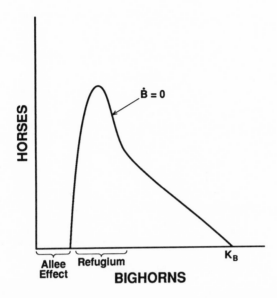

Figure 4.7. A proposed static curve for bighorn sheep illustrating all combinations of B and H where B' = 0. The hump is attributed to a partial refugium from horses in precipitous terrain where horses are unlikely to forage. The carrying capacity for bighorn sheep is depicted K_B.

ing to Hall (1972), but are still more than four times as large as adult bighorn sheep where females average 56 kg and males 74 kg (Thorne et al. 1979). Given these differences in body mass, interspecific competition coefficients are not likely to be symmetrical. We have postulated competition coefficients a = 3.2 and f = 0.2.

Our model results suggest that selective culling of horses and bighorn sheep can be manipulated to ensure coexistence of both species on the BICA. The model also makes the common-sense prediction that a greater cull of horses can enhance the sheep population. Finally, model predictions reinforce our concern that hunting of bighorn sheep may reduce the population below the level necessary to sustain a viable population.

RESEARCH NEEDS

Many of the parameter inputs that we employed in our modeling exercise were crude estimates that need to be refined for reliable predictions. To doc-

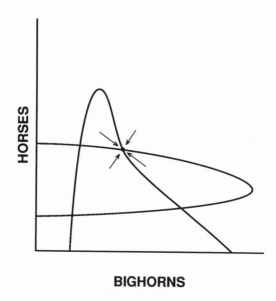

BIGHORNS

Figure 4.8. Combining static population isoclines for bighorn sheep and horses results in predicted equilibrium competitive interaction between the two species indicated by the arrows. The other three intersection points are unstable saddle points.

ument the dynamics of the interaction between bighorn sheep and horses, diets of bighorn sheep and horses need to be monitored. Moreover, research should be conducted to assess the effects that these animals are having on plant communities on the BICA. At this stage, the potential for competition between bighorn sheep and horses is conjecture based upon shared water sources and diet. Verification of this conjecture will probably require experimental manipulations; for example, with captive animals in paddocks.

To refine estimates of effective population size for bighorn sheep, we must have better estimates of the variance in reproductive success among bighorn sheep rams (see, for example, Hogg 1984). It will also be interesting to explore whether habitat segregation between male and female sheep render one sex or the other more susceptible to competition with feral horses.

Hall (1972) notes that most of the horse range lies within critical mule deer (*Odocoileus hemionus*) winter range, and that horses may compete with deer. However, horses seldom use mountain mahogany, which appears to be the preferred forage for mule deer. Research is also needed to determine the degree and nature of competition between horses and mule deer.

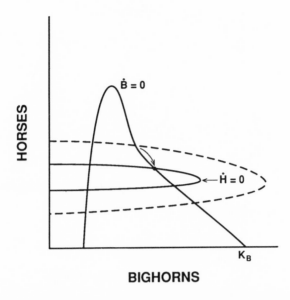

BIGHORNS

Figure 4.9. Here we depict the consequences of moderate culling on the horse population. Note that the equilibrium population size increases for the bighorns, but decreases for the horses. If culling on the horse population were even more severe, one can envisage the horse population being driven to extinction and equilibrium occurring at K_B.

MANAGEMENT CONSIDERATIONS

With proper management, coexistence of bighorn sheep and horses likely can be sustained on the BICA and PMWHR. To achieve this objective, existing evidence suggests that bighorn sheep hunting should not be permitted on the Bighorn Canyon National Recreation Area until the sheep population has attained a minimum of 125 to 150 individuals. This population size may be achieved within a couple of years if the population growth rate remains high. Already, two hunting permits for mature rams have been issued for the fall of 1990 by the Montana Department of Fish, Wildlife and Parks. Removal of mature rams further requires an increase in total population size necessary to achieve a minimum effective population base of fifty sheep.

A clear result of our modeling exercise is that a culling program for horses must be maintained to ensure coexistence of bighorns and horses, despite an apparent conflict with proposed wilderness management for a portion of the area. This also has important management ramifications because, at the time of this writing, the state director of the BLM has not authorized funding for a

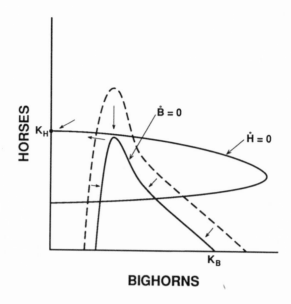

Figure 4.10. In this diagram we show how culling could likewise reduce the isocline for bighorn sheep, potentially destabilizing the system. This could result in the extinction of the sheep population and equilibrium being reached at K_H.

1990 horse roundup. The BLM-recommended population of 121 horses may need to be reduced in view of the recent competition for forage resources with bighorn sheep.

One of the justifications for maintaining horses on western wildlands is that horses were present during the Pleistocene, but became extinct due to overexploitation by man (Martin 1981, Fletcher and Warren 1988). Therefore, restocking with horses should be considered faunal recovery rather than invasion by an exotic. We cannot accept this rationale because we have no information on the ecological requirements of the extinct Pleistocene equids of North America. They were most certainly different species with different requirements from those of the feral horses of today. Furthermore, there is no clear evidence that man caused the extinction of Pleistocene equids. Indeed, evidence exists that both favors and contradicts the Pleistocene overkill hypothesis (Martin 1967, Boyce and Boyce 1976).

The National Park Service retains greater flexibility in the management of national recreation areas than for national parks. For example, recreational uses such as hunting and fishing are actually encouraged on some national recreation areas. As it relates to exotic species, National Park Service policy states that in places zoned as natural areas, "Non-native species of plants and animals will be eliminated where it is possible to do so by approved methods which will preserve wilderness qualities." Natural areas of the BICA designated as wild horse range are subzoned for "wildlife preservation" (National Park Service 1981).

Policy on the management of wilderness areas must take account of societal as well as scientific priorities. Clearly, there is a large public that desires an opportunity to observe feral horses in a wilderness setting. It is a personal judgment call as to whether the occurrence of feral horses or the culling of horses are consistent with wilderness values.

For many exotic mammals, it is difficult if not impossible to control the species (Usher 1989). Here, our ability to control the species is not in question; rather, it is a question of social values which actually prefer that the exotic species be maintained. It remains to be seen whether the federal government will give priority for management of wilderness values including native taxa, or for the perpetuation of a pasture for exotic feral horses. With careful, enlightened management, we can expect to have both.

ACKNOWLEDGMENTS

We thank Kevin Coates for stimulating our interest in this problem. John Dennis gave us insight into National Park Service policy on exotic species. Thanks to Joel Berger, William G. Binnewies, and Gary K. Howe for reviewing the manuscript.

REFERENCES

Becklund, W. W., and M. L. Walker. 1969. "Taxonomy, Hosts and Geographic Distribution of the *Setaria* (Nematoda: Filarioidea) in the U.S.A. and Canada." *Journal of Parasitology* 55:359–368.

Berger, J. 1977. "Sympatric and Allopatric Relationships among Desert Bighorn Sheep and Feral Equids in Grand Canyon." *Southwestern Naturalist* 22:540–543.

———. 1985. "Interspecific Interactions and Dominance among Wild Great Basin, USA, Ungulates." *Journal of Mammalogy* 66:571–573.

———. 1986. *Wild Horses of the Great Basin: Social Competition and Population Size.* Chicago: University of Chicago Press.

———. 1990. "Persistence of Different-sized Populations: An Empirical Assessment of Rapid Extinctions in Bighorn Sheep." *Conservation Biology* 4:91–98.

Boyce, M. S., and J. J. Boyce. 1976. "Pleistocene extinctions." *Science* 191:102.

Caughley, G. 1979. "What is This Thing Called Carrying Capacity?" In M. S. Boyce and L. D. Hayden-Wing (eds.) *North American Elk: Ecology, Behavior and Management.* Laramie: University of Wyoming.

Coates, K. P., and S. D. Schemnitz. 1989. *The Bighorn Sheep of Bighorn Canyon National Recreation Area and Pryor Mountain Wild Horse Range: Ecological Relationships and Management Recommendations.* Lovell, Wo.: Final Report to Bighorn Canyon National Recreation Area.

Coates, K. P., S. D. Schemnitz, and J. T. Peters. 1988. "Effect of Interspecific Disturbance on Foraging Behavior of Bighorn Sheep at a Wild Horse Range." *Biennial Symposium of the Northern Wild Sheep and Goat Council* 6:268.

Demarchi, D. A., and H. B. Mitchell. 1973. "The Chilcotin River Bighorn Population." *Canadian Field-Naturalist* 87:433–454.

Dennis, J. G. 1980. "National Park Service Research on Exotic Species and the Policy behind that Research: An Introduction to the Special Session on Exotic Species." In *Proceedings of the Second Conference on Scientific Research in National Parks, 26–30 November 1979,* San Francisco, Calif. pp. 241–252.

Derrick, W., and L. H. Metzgar. 1991. "Zero Growth Isoclines for Exploited Competitors." *Journal of Theoretical Biology* (in press).

Fletcher, M. R., and M. C. Warren. 1988. "African oryx (*Oryx gazella*) at White Sands National Monument." In L. K. Thomas (ed.) *Management of Exotic Species in Natural Communities.* Proceedings of a Conference on Science in the National Parks, Vol. 5. Fort Collins, Colo.: The George Wright Society, pp. 11–13.

Ganskopp, D., and M. Vavra. 1987. "Slope Use by Cattle, Feral Horses, Deer and Bighorn Sheep." *Northwest Science* 61:74–81.

Garrott, R. A., and L. Taylor. 1990. "Dynamics of a Feral Horse Population in Montana." *Journal of Wildlife Management* 54:603–612.

Gausse, G. F. 1935. *Verifications experimentales de la theorie mathematique de la lutte pour la vie.* Actualites scientifiques et industrielles, 277. Paris: Hermann.

Geist, V. 1971. *Mountain Sheep: A Study in Behavior and Evolution.* Chicago: University of Chicago Press.

Hall, R. 1972. *Wild Horse: Biology and Alternatives for Management, Pryor Mountain Horse Range.* Billings, Mont.: U.S. Bureau of Land Management.

Hamilton, W. D. 1971. "Geometry for the Selfish Herd." *Journal of Theoretical Biology* 31:295–311.

Hansen, R. M., and R. C. Clark. 1977. "Foods of Elk and Other Ungulates at Low Elevations in Northwestern Colorado." *Journal of Wildlife Management* 41:76–80.

Harris, R. B., and F. W. Allendorf. 1990. "Genetically Effective Population Size of Large Mammals: An Assessment of Estimators." *Conservation Biology* 3:181–191.

Hobbs, N. T., M. W. Miller, J. A. Bailey, D. F. Reed, and R. B. Gill. 1990. "Biological Criteria for Introductions of Large Mammals: Using Simulation Models to Predict Impacts of Competition." *Transactions of the North American Wildlife and Natural Resources Conference* 55:620–632.

Hogg, J. T. 1984. "Mating in Bighorn Sheep: Multiple Creative Male Strategies." *Science* 225:526–529.

Hutchinson, G. E. 1965. *The Ecological Theater and the Evolutionary Play.* New Haven, Conn.: Yale University Press.

Knight, D. H., G. P. Jones, Y. Akashi, and R. W. Myers. 1987. *Vegetation Ecology in the Bighorn Canyon National Recreation Area.* Final Report. Laramie: University of Wyoming-National Park Service Research Center.

LaCava, J., and J. Hughes. 1984. "Determining Minimum Viable Population Levels." *Wildlife Society Bulletin* 12:370–376.

Lange, R. E., A. V. Sandoval, and W. P. Meleney. 1980. "Psoroptic Scabies in Bighorn Sheep, *Ovis canadensis mexicana* in New Mexico, U.S.A." *Journal of Wildlife Diseases* 16:77–82.

Lotka, A. J. 1925. *Elements of Physical Biology.* New York: Dover, 1956.

Martin, P. S. 1967. *Pleistocene Extinctions.* New Haven, Conn.: Yale University Press.

Metzgar, L. H., and E. Boyd. 1988. "Stability Properties in a Model of Forage-Ungulate-Predator Interactions." *Natural Resource Modeling* 3:3–43.

National Park Service. 1981. *Final General Management Plan for the Bighorn Canyon National Recreation Area.* Denver: U.S. Department of the Interior, Denver Service Center.

National Research Council. 1982. *Wild and Free-roaming Horses and Burros.* Washington, D.C.: National Academy Press.

Paine, R. T. 1966. "Food Web Complexity and Species Diversity." *American Naturalist* 100:65–76.

Rosenzweig, M. L. 1969. "Why the Prey Curve Has a Hump." *American Naturalist* 103:81–87.

Sausman, K. A. 1984. "Survival of Captive-born *Ovis canadensis* in North American Zoos." *Zoo Biology* 3:111–121.

Soulé, M. E. 1980. "Thresholds for Survival: Maintaining Fitness and Evolutionary Potential." In M. E. Soulé and B. A. Wilcox (eds.) *Conservation Biology: An Evolutionary-Ecological Perspective.* Sunderland, Mass.: Sinauer Associates.

Thorne, E. T., G. Butler, T. Varcalli, K. Becker, and S. Hayden-Wing. 1979. *The Status, Mortality and Response to Management of the Bighorn Sheep of Whiskey Mountain.* Cheyenne: Wyoming Game and Fish Department, Wildlife Technical Report No. 7.

U.S. Bureau of Land Management. 1984. *Herd Management Area Plan: Pryor Mountain Wild Horse Range.* Miles City, Mont.: U.S. Department of the Interior, Bureau of Land Management.

Usher, M. B. 1989. "Ecological Effects of Controlling Invasive Terrestrial Vertebrates." In J. A. Drake et al. (eds.) *Biological Invasions: A Global Perspective, Scope 37.* New York: J. Wiley, pp. 463–490.

Volterra, V. 1926. "Fluctuations in the Abundance of a Species Considered Mathematically." *Nature* 118:558–560.

Wright, S. 1931. "Evolution in Mendelian populations." *Genetics* 16:97–109.

Yodzis, P. 1976. "The Effects of Harvesting on Competitive Systems." *Bulletin of Mathematical Biology* 38:97–109.

———. 1989. *Introduction to Theoretical Ecology.* New York: Harper and Row.

5

AQUATIC RESOURCES OF THE ARID WEST: PERSPECTIVES ON FISHES AND WILDERNESS MANAGEMENT

John W. Sigler and William F. Sigler

INTRODUCTION

Floods: "For forty days the flood kept coming on the earth and as the waters increased, they lifted the ark high above the earth. The waters rose and increased greatly on the earth . . . the waters rose and covered the mountains" (Genesis 7:17-20 NIV).

Drought: "Sometime later the brook dried up because there had been no rain in the land" (1 Kings 17:7 NIV).

Difficulties with water management (that is, water resources utilization) are obviously not new to mankind. Residents of the western interior deserts are no strangers to water crises. During the 1980s, Utah, Nevada, Arizona, New Mexico, and parts of California and Idaho experienced snowpack and subsequent flood waters in excess of 200% of normal (1983 to 1985). Severe weather conditions resulted in such novel occurrences as the "State Street River": State Street in downtown Salt Lake City, Utah, was sandbagged and turned into a conduit for the excess flood waters coming off the mountains of the Wasatch Front. These conditions also resulted in the expenditure of more than eighty million dollars to install a pumping station on the west edge of Great Salt Lake to move excess waters into the desert west of the lake to relieve the massive flooding occurring along its developed shores. Streams such as the pluvial White River in Nevada, which are, under normal precipitation regimes, a series of discontinuous and isolated aquatic ecosystems (potholes), ran from their headwaters to their mouths for the first time in recent history. This caused great consternation among fisheries scientists and managers concerned with the protection of unique fish species occurring in these secluded and disjunct pothole ecosystems.

By 1988 and 1989 water conditions had reversed 180 degrees. The Utah legislature and the governor convened a Bear River Legislative Task Force to study ways to dam the waters of the Bear River in northern Utah to alleviate severe droughts and water shortages affecting the state's northern counties and their agricultural base. Authorization for the expenditure of several thousand dollars to document the need, priority, and location of one or more dams on the Bear River and its tributaries underscored the severity of the anticipated water shortage. Farmers and ranchers elsewhere in the interior western deserts began the process of recovering lands for grazing and crops that had been inundated for up to five years. Recovery plans for such areas as the Bear River Migratory Waterfowl Refuge below Brigham City, Utah, inundated by the rising waters of the Great Salt Lake, were developed to reclaim the marshes as the flood waters receded.

What these two extreme and contrasting situations accentuate is the prevalence of water crises in the western deserts: frequent now, they may be continual by the end of this century. The ability and the need to move water from areas of excess (even during flood events) to areas of relative shortage (even in drought periods) are likely to become an essential component of state, local, and federal water management practices in the twenty-first century.

One need look no farther than the Central Utah Project (CUP) or the Central Arizona Project (CAP)—which have proposed and implemented transbasin water movements on a mammoth scale—to appreciate the ability of humans to change the face of the earth with respect to water resources. These existing and potential water development (read: *water dependent*) projects add an additional threat to the ecological well-being of the desert's water resources, including, but not limited to, native fishes as well as those introduced. In the face of continued water management, western desert aquatic ecosystems are both a treasure to be protected and a resource to be utilized with wise stewardship.

Desert aquatic ecosystems, and the unique endemic species they support, are fragile. While both the physical ecosystem components and the associated flora and fauna have withstood thousands of years of climatic and geologic change, their long histories have not conditioned them to sudden man-made changes.

Wilderness areas, by definition, are not overcrowded by humans or their accoutrements of civilization. They are remote, relatively inaccessible, foreboding (to some), or some combination of these or other factors that all discourage heavy use. Aquatic ecosystems in these areas are protected by these characteristics and, in turn, contribute to the nature of the area's resource values. Further attributes of desert wilderness in general, as well as specific examples of these unique areas, are presented in Chapter 7 in this volume.

DESERTS AND DESERT ECOSYSTEMS

There is no consensus definition of a desert. Deserts have been defined in terms of the vegetation types, soils, and variability in climatic factors. A reasonable set of factors around which to build a definition would include: the amount of precipitation received, the distribution of this precipitation over a calendar year, the amount of evaporation, the mean temperature during a designated period, and the amount and utilization of the solar radiation received (Bender 1982). Miller (1981) suggests one parameter that defines a desert: where annual precipitation is generally less than 250 to 300 mm. More complex formula definitions, as presented by Bender (1982), include de Martone's "Aridity Index" and Budyko's Radiational Index of Dryness. *Webster's Collegiate Dictionary's* definition of desert includes the conceptual aspects of a solitary waste area—uninhabited, dry, barren, and treeless. An ecological definition embodies the concepts of restricted species diversity, severe climatic conditions, and unpredictable resource allocation (for example, water input). To most people, a desert is simply an area that is generally hot and dry.

Another method of defining inland deserts is by contrast. Arizona, Nevada, New Mexico, Utah, and parts of California, Idaho, and Oregon all are considered deserts. Arizona has a record high temperature of 53°C, an average July temperature of 27°C, an average January temperature of 5°C, and an average annual precipitation of 33 cm. Utah, considered the second driest state, has a record high temperature of 47°C, an average July temperature of 23°C, average January temperature of −4°C, and an average annual precipitation of 30 cm. Other states in the region share similar parameters. (Average precipitation figures, however, are misleading. The majority of precipitation falls in higher mountain altitudes as snow or rain in the winter months. While some areas receive twice the average, many lower elevation areas receive half or less than half the average precipitation. Additionally, the evaporation rate in desert areas where water accumulates may be more than one meter per year, decreasing the availability of water that falls as precipitation [Sigler et al. 1983].) Mississippi, on the other hand, has a record high temperature of 45°C, average July temperatures of 27°C, average January temperatures of 8°C, and an average annual precipitation of 142 cm. Furthermore, Florida and Washington state, also perceived to be areas of high precipitation, have mean annual precipitation totals that are as much as an order of magnitude higher than those for the desert states (*World Book Encyclopedia* 1988).

Other comparisons to be made include the number of fish species (or other aquatic life forms) present in a state and the number native to that geographic area. Utah lists sixty-four species, only twenty-seven of which are native (Sigler et al. 1992). Arizona lists ninety-nine species, many of which are non-native (Minckley 1973). Similar numbers represent species diversity in the other western desert states. By contrast, Missouri lists twenty-five families and dozens of species, most of which are native (Pfleiger 1975). Protected fish species, those afforded status as threatened or endangered under the federal Endangered Species Act, also reflect the differences in aquatic fauna richness. Arizona has eight protected species, seventeen of special concern; Nevada has twenty-three protected species, nineteen of special concern; and Utah has thirteen protected, one of special concern. By contrast, Missouri, a state with far more species, has nine protected and twenty-seven of special concern. Florida has sixteen protected species, and Washington state has but eleven species of special concern (Johnson 1987). The functional differences between states that have diverse and abundant fish or other aquatic fauna and states that have a relatively depauperate fish or aquatic fauna are simply diversity and richness of habitat. (See Appendix for a list of fishes discussed here.)

PHYSICAL HABITAT AND BIOLOGICAL ADAPTATIONS

Physical Habitat

Arid regions of the western United States are not unique, but many are definitely different from those in other parts of the country. As noted above, rainfall is minimal, so understandably the terrestrial vegetation is sparse (Naiman 1981). Much of the Great Basin is dominated by shrubs, particularly sagebrush (*Artemisia tridentata*), but before the arrival of the livestock man and the great herds of cattle and lesser numbers of sheep, many of the western arid lands supported a plant cover of native bunch grasses and shrubs, which protected the fragile land from wind and water erosion. The live grasses protected the land in the spring and summer, and the shrubs and plant residue provided protection in fall and winter. Many of the large erosion gullies of today appeared only after the protective plant cover had been badly depleted by overgrazing. Overgrazing and other terrestrial ecosystem abuses led to impacts (siltation, bank erosion, sloughing) which were transferred to the aquatic ecosystems by climatic and geologic processes. Impacted aquatic ecosystems have not recovered, and will not recover until the terrestrial ecosystems of which they are a functional counterpart have been rehabilitated or at least stabilized. Recovery of these impacted terrestrial ecosystems is slow, often requiring decades. Such damage and recovery processes reflect both overuse and the lack of consistent water supplies.

Desert Streams

Desert aquatic ecosystems are often violent, severe environs, subject to both rapid change, as well as extremes of temperature on an annual (55°C to below O°C) or diurnal (air temperature fluctuations of perhaps 30°C) basis. These natural and cyclic fluctuations are part of the evolutionary development of the aquatic species inhabiting them. Only when the fluctuations exceed the geologic time norm do species fail to cope.

Desert streams are fed largely from rainfall, which may come by way of violent thunderstorms, or, in some instances, as torrents raging through arroyos. Sheep Creek, in the Uinta Mountains of eastern Utah, flooded June 11, 1965, and carried 27 m pine trees and 2.4 m boulders from high up in the mountains out to an alfalfa field in the valley. Picnic tables farther downstream were half buried in sand and silt, a delivery truck was mired to its 3 m top, and a family of six campers was never seen again. In the early 1950s a group of biologists were crossing a small dry arroyo, driving on a road below the Henry Mountains in southeastern Utah. They looked up to see a 3 to 4 m high wall of water carrying a large tree bearing down on them. They were barely out of the arroyo when the wall of water crashed by them. Later, on a wide sandy flat they came to a river about 1.6 km wide. In thirty minutes it was gone. These events reflect the tenuous and violent nature of desert ecosystems within which aquatic organisms must survive.

Disjunct Aquatic Ecosystems (Potholes)

Aquifer-fed ponds, or potholes, as opposed to streams, are little affected by rainfall; they have a relatively stable environment. The water chemistry of these ponds is reasonably constant: the physical changes, including temperature, are slow and moderate. However, Constantz (1981) suggests that "constant condition" springs may be less predictable than fluctuating desert arroyos. In such spring environments, fish may be born at a time of either high or low food production, or on either end of any of a number of physical cycles. Constantz feels that a stream environment thus may be more predictable and constant than a spring. The diversity of species of both plants and animals in springs is low, and the species of fish found in springs and streams predictably are quite different. The growing season in the desert is long, the number of very warm to hot days is high, and evaporation is high—all factors which may have ecological effects on pothole ecosystems. Desert conditions discourage many species, but others have adapted and not only survive but prosper.

Biological Adaptations

Life History Adaptations

The timing and duration of breeding strategies in desert fishes varies dramatically between species and, in most cases, are dictated by both life span and specific habitat conditions. For example, the Devils Hole pupfish and the Amargosa pupfish, which are found in near-constant-temperature spring environments, live a maximum of two to three years and typically breed year-round in very restricted spatial environments. The Amargosa pupfish has been known to produce as many as eight to ten broods per year. In contrast, the Colorado squawfish, of the main-stem Colorado River, lives from twelve to fifteen years and confines its breeding activities to a three- to four-week period each year. The Colorado squawfish historically migrated to spawn over comparatively large distances and may not have spawned until six to seven years of age.

The original habitat of the Devils Hole pupfish is a 7 m by 2.7 m rockbound pool in Ash Meadows, Nevada. It is connected to a largely unexplored subterranean reservoir, but the pupfish spends much of its time along a shallow shelf of about 19 square meters (Baugh and Deacon 1983). The existence of this endemic species, and its entire life history are intricately linked to an area not much larger than most American living rooms.

Morphological Adaptations

Spring fishes are chubby with rounded fins; they can maintain position in slow currents or in still water. Stream fishes have fusiform bodies and long pointed fins. A special body form adaption is present in certain of the Colorado River fast-water fishes. The humpback chub, the Colorado squawfish, and the razorback sucker have somewhat flattened heads. Two of the three have pronounced nuchal humps, and two have long slender caudal peduncles (Sigler and Miller 1963, Constantz 1981).

The chiselmouth, a 25 to 30 cm minnow, and the only living species in its genus, feeds by scraping periphyton off rocks with its chisellike lower jaw. This morphological adaptation allows the chiselmouth to exploit a niche within its habitat (for example, by scraping diatomaceous algae off rocks or other substrates) virtually without competition from other species.

Physiological Adaptations

Western mosquito fish, in a spring southeast of Malad, Idaho, survived and reproduced in a 1 meter band of 42°C water. No other species of fish can tolerate the even lower temperatures, allowing the mosquito fish to exploit this niche without competition. However, even this species could not venture into the center of the pond where it was 49°C.

The Arctic grayling starts its spawning run among the spring ice floes, but does not prosper in temperatures much above 13°C. The Amargosa pupfish, in the Amargosa River, Nevada–California, live in waters that range from near freezing to 40°C; it also prospers in freshwater springs in Nye County, Nevada, that range from 21 to 33°C, but vary no more than 2 to 7°C (Sigler and Sigler 1987).

Before the advent of non–native Americans, fishes of the Colorado River system—notably the bonytail, humpback, and roundtail chubs—and the squaw-fish and razorback sucker adapted to extremes of flow in the magnitude of several hundred percent, with temperatures ranging from near freezing to over 38°C, and from high turbidity to nearly clear water.

The Lahontan cutthroat trout, cui-ui, Tahoe sucker, tui chub, and Sacramento perch in terminal high desert Pyramid Lake, Nevada, have developed a tolerance for, and seem to prosper in, total dissolved solids of 5.5 ppt, or more.

HABITAT LOSSES OR DESTRUCTION

The advance of early-day industry and agriculture across the western United States was, almost without exception, synonymous with some degree of native fish habitat destruction. Habitat was either decreased or degraded, often both. Exotic fishes were introduced that both outcompeted, preyed on, or carried new diseases to native species.

Stream Habitats

In the mid-nineteenth century, Utah pioneers quickly turned to Utah Lake for a ready and abundant source of high protein food in the form of native fishes. In spite of some regulations, commercial fishing was virtually unre-stricted. There appeared to be an endless supply of Bonneville cutthroat trout, Utah sucker, and June sucker. There was also a sculpin, which is generally considered to be an indicator of high-quality water. Intense agricultural activ-ities soon began to degrade water quality, a predictable and almost inevita-ble circumstance where crops of the arid West thrive only through irrigation. The cutthroat was the first species to disappear; then, in the drought years of the mid-1930s, the original June sucker and the Utah Lake sculpin also dis-appeared. Only the Utah sucker, a highly adaptable species, survived. Deg-radation of habitat, rather than overfishing, eventually struck the fatal blow for the cutthroat trout, the June sucker, and the sculpin.

The Newlands Project, completed in 1905 in western Nevada, was the first federal irrigation system in the United States. Its transbasin diversion of water from the Truckee River to the Carson River essentially spelled the end of the once world-famous original Lahontan cutthroat trout fishery in Pyramid Lake. Derby Dam, built on the Truckee River above Pyramid Lake, reduced the range of the cutthroat from 193 km in the main stem of the river, plus proba-bly another 95 tributary km, to the often low and sometimes dry 48 km between the dam and the lake. It also excluded Lake Tahoe and its tributaries as Lahontan cutthroat habitat. The world's largest cutthroat, though doomed, managed to hang on until 1938, with a few still reported in 1943 (Sigler et al. 1983). The system now supports one endangered (cui-ui) and one threatened (Lahontan cutthroat trout) species (Sigler and Sigler 1987).

In the Colorado River system today, three native fishes are endangered, and one is being considered for protected status. These are the Colorado squawfish, the humpback chub, the bonytail chub, and the razorback sucker. Most other native fishes have been drastically reduced in number.

The Colorado River is one of the largest and most beautiful rivers in western North America. Its origin is high in the Rocky Mountains in northern Colorado, fed by snow from 4270 m peaks, and flows for 2190 km southwest into the Gulf of California. The watershed covers 629,000 square km. Before the coming of the white man and his extensive alterations for dams and irrigation or hydroelectric projects, flows ranged from extremely high flood conditions to extreme low flow during drought. Temperatures varied from very cold water in the Rockies, even in summer, to over 38°C in the lower reaches (Arizona). Today, the river system has so many dams and diversions that much of it only remotely resembles the original river. The most notable exception is the Grand Canyon, and even here flows are much reduced and daily release cycles, regulated by the hydroelectric complex of Glen Canyon Dam, cause surge flows with accompanying beach erosion throughout the canyon. The four above named, once abundant native fishes, evolving over thousands of years, were adapted to this muddy, turbulent, fast, and cool to warm river. Then came the dams creating large placid, stratified lakes, with clear, coldwater streams below. The change was too drastic and too rapid for them; they could not adjust. Today, only a few declining numbers remain.

Disjunct Aquatic Ecosystems (Potholes)

The Devils Hole pupfish of Devil's Hole, Ash Meadows, Nevada, lives in a very small pool that has a small shallow shelf where the fish breeds. A drop in water level large enough to expose the shelf would terminate reproduction, leading to the extinction of this endemic species. When early developers started pumping nearby aquifers, it led to a lowering of the water level in Devil's Hole. In a landmark decision by the United States Supreme Court, the pumping operation was ordered terminated to preserve the habitat of this unique species. Devil's Hole is now a disjunct segment of Death Valley National Monument.

ECOSYSTEM AND RESOURCE UTILIZATION

It is often argued that fishing in the arid West is much better because of certain fishes introduced from the eastern United States and elsewhere. This

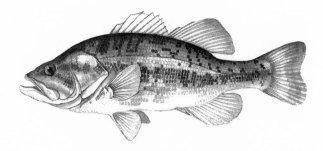

Figure 5.1. Largemouth bass. *Micropterus salmoides* (Lacepède).

is undoubtedly true, but largely because of man-made changes in the aquatic environment. These changes reduced native species, and created habitat better suited to introduced fish species. The Colorado River system offers the best example of the type of changes that have occurred typically. Flaming Gorge Lake on the Green River is much better suited to lake trout, brown trout, and kokanee than it is to native cutthroat. Lake Powell and the other downstream lakes are better suited to largemouth bass (Figure 5.1), black crappie, bluegill, and striped bass than to any native species. With extensively and drastically altered habitat, exotics often become a necessity to achieve acceptable levels of fishing success. This is not to suggest that all introductions have a positive impact, nor does it mean that certain exotics in an undergraded habitat might not have improved fishing success.

The common carp (Figure 5.2) is often used as an example of a stocking that should not have happened. It is generally shunned by anglers; and in western waterfowl marshes, where it flourishes, it is at times highly destructive. The rationale for the original stockings of carp were explained in reports of regional and national fishery managers during the late 1800s (original citations in Sigler and Sigler 1987).

> Common carp was one of the most frequently introduced fish. It was brought into the United States by Rudolph Hessel. Utah received its first shipment of fish from the Washington, D.C. U.S. Fish station in 1881 and H. G. Parker, the first Fish Commissioner of Nevada, in his 1878 report to the governor expressed his intent to stock the waters of the state with this "superior food fish." A mere decade later, when George Mills became the third Fish Commissioner of Nevada, Mr. Mills made public his sentiment regarding carp by stating ". . . the general government, while not entirely to blame, was "particpet criminis" in foisting upon this state, and in polluting our waters with, that undesirable fish the carp . . . Time has now established its worthlessness and our waters are suffering their presence."

In Utah there are now twenty-seven native species and thirty-seven introduced species (Sigler et al. 1992). Of the thirty-seven species, ten at most

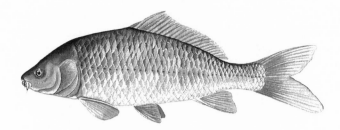

Figure 5.2. Common carp. *Cyprinus carpio* Linnaeus.

can be said to have substantial positive benefits with respect to recreational fishing. The others have slight benefits or are either neutral or negative. In the Great Basin, one-half of the eighty-eight species are native. In some instances, policies for stocking fish are set without sufficient knowledge of how a given species will respond to a foreign environment, or more importantly, how native aquatic organisms will respond to the introduction.

HABITATS AND REPRESENTATIVE FISH SPECIES

Below we characterize selected desert aquatic habitat types and the fish species found in, or representative of, those types. In each case, the organisms have evolved over hundreds, if not thousands, of years, and their faunal and physiographic relationships are tied to either geologic events or specific locations such as Pleistocene Lake Bonneville in Utah or Lake Lahontan in Nevada. In these locations, many remnant endemic populations exist (Minckley et al. 1986). The relict dace serves as a good general example: evolving 1.5 to 2 million years ago, its habitat was relatively constant from the time of desiccation of Pleistocene Lake Lahontan some 10,000 years ago until the entry of European people into the Great Basin in the late 1700s. The life histories, included below, and the ecological conditions in which the species exist are reflections of the severity, diversity, and uniqueness of desert aquatic ecosystems.

Spring and Small Stream Habitats

Killifishes (Family Cyprinodontidae) are representative spring and small-stream fishes. Family distribution ranges nearly worldwide in temperate and tropical climates. The killifishes are small, highly colored, and generally sexually dimorphic. They are adapted to surface feeding by a flattened head and a mouth that opens near the upper surface. These fish are oviparous.

Habitat features of killifish ecosystems include relatively stable temperatures in many instances and small, disjunct ecosystems. A particular species of killifish may be the only fish species present in some locations. The ecological concept of spring or spring areas as "islands" is valid here (Sigler and Sigler 1986).

White River Springfish

The White River springfish is present in several warm springs in the now disrupted pluvial White River of eastern Nevada. The temperature of these springs ranges from 21 to 37°C, and the biological oxygen demand (BOD) is moderately high. This species is omnivorous in June, but plants, primarily filamentous algae, are its most important foods. Later, it remains primarily herbivorous, but also feeds on caddisfly larvae. Breeding extends through the summer. There are ten to fifteen eggs produced at each individual spawning. Eggs hatch in about a week at average summer temperatures. Fish reach a size of about 5 cm. A few may live three or more years. Habitat degradation and the introduction of exotic fishes are negative factors which continue to pose a threat to its survival (Deacon et al. 1980).

Owens Pupfish

The Owens pupfish was once abundant in the Owens River system in California. Limited numbers are now present near Lone Pine and at Fish Slough in Mono County, California. Clear shallow water with a few deep pools, temperatures of 10 to 24°C, *Chara* spp., and emergent bulrushes constitute the preferred habitat. This species is predaceous on mosquito larvae, midge larvae, mayflies, and beetles. It may be a more effective predator on mosquito larvae than mosquito fish. It spawns in summer when temperatures hover around 20°C. As with other pupfishes, the male guards an area, and eggs are laid and fertilized singly. One female may produce several hundred eggs in a year. A few individuals may live more than two years, but most live less. It is generally not over 5 cm long. In the early days, when Owens River water was first allotted for out-of-channel use, the fish lost habitat and was greatly reduced in numbers (Kennedy 1916, Miller and Pister 1971).

Salt Creek Pupfish

The original range of the Salt Creek pupfish is Salt Creek and Cottonball Marsh, all within Death Valley National Monument in California and Nevada. This fish, living 61 to 91 m below sea level, has adapted to an environment so harsh that few if any other fish could survive there. It tolerates temperatures ranging from near freezing to 42°C, total dissolved solids of 26 ppt, and water so salty that few terrestrial plants can survive. Part of the habitat is dry except during fall and spring, but the fish can retreat to small shaded pools. Salt Creek pupfish feed on algae and a variety of aquatic animals. Breeding is similar to that in other pupfishes. Their violent fluctuations in population numbers may be unique among fishes. In this relatively small habitat, the spring-early summer population has been estimated in the millions. High temperatures and a reduction in usable habitat during late summer probably reduce the population to a few thousand. This species exhibits rapid growth, very early maturity, and produces several generations in one year. A few live one year or slightly more, but most survive only a few months; maximum size is about 3.8 cm (Miller 1943).

Pahrump Killifish

The original population of this subspecies has been extirpated from Pahrump Valley, Nevada, due to habitat losses. Two transplanted populations exist in Shoshone Pond near Ely, Nevada, and in Corn Creek Springs in southwestern Nevada. The original habitat consisted of moderate-temperature small ponds with minimal fluctuations. Its food preference is apparently small invertebrates; it probably spawns in early spring, is short lived, and reaches a length of 5 cm (Deacon and Williams 1984).

Large River Habitats

Large-stream desert fishes are quite different from the killifishes. The largest river in the western desert is the Colorado. Representative fish species include members of the carp and minnows family (Family Cyprinidae), the sucker family (Family Catostomidae), and trouts (Family Salmonidae).

Habitat characteristics of these fishes include turbid, high spring runoff, fluctuating flows, and temperatures on an annual cycle. All of these fishes were commonly found with one to several other species of fish in their undisturbed native habitats.

Humpback Chub

The original range of the humpback chub is the Colorado River system. Their present range is much reduced. Agricultural and industrial development of the Colorado has reduced the number of humpback chubs to but a small remnant of their former population size. Adults have a flattened head, a prominent nuchal hump, and a streamlined body with a thin peduncle. This body form was well adapted to the fast, turbulent waters of the unaltered Colorado River. (It should be noted that even fishes adapted to fast waters spend relatively little time there.) The young frequent the quiet backwater areas or stay close to shore. The humpback feeds mostly on invertebrates, including terrestrial insects, but it will feed on vulnerable small fish. It breeds in the spring in rising water temperatures of 17 to 20°C. Breeding areas have slow water and sand-gravel bottoms. It matures at 20 to 25 cm and produces several thousand eggs. The spawning season for a population lasts three to four weeks. It reaches a size of 30 cm and lives from eight to ten years.

Colorado Squawfish

The native range of this fish is the Colorado River system, from high in Colorado and Wyoming to the Gulf of California. It is now present in only a few places, including the Upper Colorado River basin. The Colorado squawfish was abundant and well adapted to the original, wild, and turbulent river, but has not been able to adapt to the many man-made changes. It was abundant in most of the river and its many tributaries. It is probably the only truly piscivorous minnow, but also readily feeds on other vertebrates. The long pikelike body and nearly horizontal mouth make it an ideal predator even in very fast water. Maturity is at about 43 cm and from six to seven years. It spawns in the spring when water temperatures reach 14 to 21°C in tributaries over riffles, producing several thousand adhesive eggs. Originally, it reached a length of 1.8 m and a weight of 45.4 kg; today it is much smaller. It was once so abundant that it was a ready source of human as well as animal food, and even served as fertilizer. In the absence of a more traditional game fish, it was prized by Native Americans and early settlers.

Razorback Sucker

This once abundant sucker ranged over most of the Colorado River system in earlier days. Today, only a few remain. A small head and large nuchal hump made it ideally suited to the historically swift waters of the Colorado River. The young have no hump and live in more quiet waters. It was, and still is, more abundant in the lower river basin than the upper. The largest numbers of the relatively few left today are in the general vicinity of Lake Mojave. Some frequent drainage ditches and canals. Razorback suckers feed, surface to bottom, on aquatic and sometimes terrestrial invertebrates and algae. Originally, it made relatively long upstream runs to spawn in tributaries over sand and gravel bars. This passage has been eliminated by dams, high flows, and thermal barriers. Spawning is initiated early in the spring when temperatures reach about 12°C; however, optimum temperature is about 18°C. It matures at three to four years when it is 25 to 30 cm. The small adhesive eggs produced by one female may number fifty thousand or more. Originally, it reached a size of 90 cm and a weight of 7.3 kg; today, it is much smaller. Like the Colorado squawfish, it was sought as a source of food by Native Americans and early settlers.

Small Stream Habitats

Native fishes in small streams, today as historically, face entirely different conditions than the fish of the main-stem Colorado River system. Small-stream habitats are represented by the cyprinids.

Habitat-type characteristics include high seasonal flows, with high sediment loads that are often high in salt content. In contrast to large rivers, habitat types may include relatively shallow water but with areas of strong current.

Woundfin

The woundfin's original range is the Virgin River and Gila River basins of southwestern Utah and south-central Arizona. Much of this area is currently under consideration for designation as wilderness. Today, the woundfin is restricted to only one tributary of the Virgin River. It inhabits streams with high sediment loads and low visibility that are often high in salt content. It prospers in waters 23 to 31°C, but is stressed at 35°C. Adults seek strong current, where water is 25 to 50 cm deep and flows of 2.3 to 2.8 cm/sec seem to be optimal. The young are found in quiet, shallow waters. Woundfins prefer little or no vegetation. This little fish is omnivorous and opportunistic, feeding on algae and aquatic, and occasionally terrestrial, invertebrates. It exhibits breeding tendencies when spring temperatures reach 14°C in April or early May. The upper limit for spawning and larval survival is 30°C. It spawns in small areas of shallow water. A few individuals reach a length of 9 cm and live three years, but most live two years or less. The most limiting factors are the drying of a large part of the habitat and the introduction of red shiner, both of which have led to a dramatic decrease in range and population numbers in the Virgin River (Deacon, J. E. 1977 unpublished manuscript, LaRivers 1962, Sigler and Miller 1963).

Virgin River Spinedace

The Virgin River spinedace's original range is the Virgin River, its tributaries in Utah, Arizona, and Nevada, and a small spring near Panaca, Nevada. Today, it is present only in a few tributaries of the Virgin River. It is one of a unique group of six New World spiny-rayed minnows that are confined to the Colorado River drainage. The dorsal fin has two smooth spines, and the pelvic fins have spinelike modifications. This subspecies prefers to be near vegetation and over sand and gravel bottoms. It seeks relatively slow, clear water about 1 m deep and near cover, at about 29°C. The Virgin River spinedace is omnivorous, feeding on aquatic and terrestrial invertebrates and plants. At the age of one year it breeds for a short time in the spring, when water temperatures are 13 to 17°C. It reaches a length of 13 cm, and lives no more than three years (Sigler and Miller 1963, Cross 1975).

Natural Lake Habitats

Trouts are representative of natural lake and stream habitats. Size variations among this family are considerable; historically, cutthroat trout reportedly reached weights of 27 kg, while the Bonneville cisco may attain a weight of only 71 grams. Trouts occur in a variety of habitats including lakes and streams, as well as man-made impoundments and large rivers. They occur over a wide range of elevations.

Habitat features of salmonid ecosystems include cold to cool and clear, well-oxygenated water. Lakes in which they are found are typically oligotrophic and streams may range from high to low gradients. In many instances, trouts, particularly cutthroat, occur where forage fish (often cyprinids) are abundant.

Bear Lake (but not its tributaries), in Utah and Idaho, appears to be one body of water that has suffered less than usual by human intervention. Since 1912, it has been used as a storage reservoir to regulate downstream flows. Meeting downstream irrigation demands in drought years can cause abnormally low water levels. There is some indication that the regulated inflow–outflow regime of Bear River water may be reducing nutrient levels in the lake. The areas available in tributary streams for the original cutthroat have been greatly reduced by agricultural activities. Artificial reproduction is necessary to maintain even a vestige of former population numbers.

Bonneville Whitefish

The Bonneville whitefish is one of four fishes endemic to Bear Lake. The others are the Bonneville cisco, the Bear Lake whitefish, and the Bear Lake sculpin. Bear Lake is a deep, cold, stratified lake at 1805.6 m above sea level. It is relatively clear. The Bonneville whitefish ranges throughout the lake, but is commonly in depths of 12 to 30 m. Adults frequent shallow water more often than the young. It feeds principally on chironomids and, to a lesser extent, on aquatic and terrestrial insects. Bonneville whitefish spawn from mid-February to early March in 1 to 3 m of water over rocky or sandy bottoms, when temperatures are around 7°C. Egg production is one thousand to five thousand per female. This whitefish may reach a weight of 1.8 kg, and an age of eight years (Sigler and Sigler 1987).

Bonneville Cisco

The Bonneville cisco (Figure 5.3) lives only in Bear Lake. It feeds on zooplankton, primarily *Epischura* and *Bosmina*. It may also eat chironomid larvae. Each year, hundreds of thousands of these little fish move from the depths to spawn in water 15 cm to 12 m deep. Spawning starts in mid-January and lasts about two weeks. During this period the water temperature ranges from near freezing to 5°C; four years out of five the lake is ice covered. A female

Figure 5.3. Bonneville cisco. *Prosopium gemmiferum* (Snyder).

produces 2,000 to 3,600 eggs. A large fish is 20 cm. Most live not more than seven years, though a few survive to eleven years (Sigler and Workman 1978).

SUCCESSES AND FAILURES

Two additional lake–stream fish should be mentioned. One species (and its habitat) has prospered by man-made changes, while the other has suffered.

Fish Habitat Success Story

Utah Chub

This native Utah minnow has not only survived alterations in its habitat, but appears to positively thrive in places such as fluctuating-level impoundments and small, muddy ditches. Its original range is the basin of ancient Lake Bonneville, mainly in Utah and Nevada, and part of the Snake River drainage. However, its range has been extended by numerous well-meaning people. Utah chub thrive at elevations of 1525 to 2750 m, at temperatures from 15 to 31°C, in clear or turbid water—in sloughs, ditches, reservoirs, large cold lakes, and large rivers. It feeds on both plants and animals, but it is opportunistic and omnivorous. In lakes, spring spawning starts when temperatures reach about 11°C and may continue until the water reaches 20°C. Spawning takes place in shallow water along the shore. One female may produce thirty thousand eggs. An eleven-year-old fish in Bear Lake was 56 cm long and weighed 1.4 kg. A more typical fish is 30 cm long and eight years old (Sigler and Sigler 1987).

Fish Habitat Failure Story

Cutthroat Trout

The cutthroat trout (Figure 5.4) is native to western North America, and in most places it is the only native trout. Its range has been greatly reduced by

Figure 5.4. Cutthroat trout. *Salmo clarki* Richardson.

agriculture and industrial development, and by the introduction of exotic fish species. This trout lives in streams from sea level to elevations of over 3000 m; it inhabits small, nearly sterile mountain lakes and large, highly alkaline lakes. Large ones, generally those over 1 kg, feed principally on fish and other vertebrates or large invertebrates, but if necessary, they will readily turn to invertebrates. The young feed on aquatic insects and other aquatic invertebrates. Stream-spawning runs commence in the spring when temperatures reach about 5 to 6°C. A temperature of 14°C is considered the upper safe limit for spawning and egg incubation. The hook-and-line-record cutthroat weighed 18.6 kg; much larger ones were reportedly caught historically in commercial fisheries. Twelve kilograms is considered large today. A normal life span is eight to ten years. In an undisturbed habitat, the native cutthroat are adaptable and competitive, but they are not able to adjust to a sometimes highly altered environment or an introgression by stocked exotic species (Sigler and Sigler 1987).

RESOURCE ALLOCATION

Despite what might appear to be overwhelming drawbacks for use by humans, the inland-desert states have a number of "user groups" competing for their resources. These lands are controlled by a variety of federal, state, and private entities. By far the largest landowners in these states are the American people, in the form of the federal government. Each of the western states has a variety of both federal and state resource management agencies. Arizona has two national parks, five national wildlife refuges, and six national forests. Nevada has one national park, five national wildlife refuges, and two national forests. Utah has five national parks, two national wildlife refuges, and six national forests. New Mexico has one national park, five national wildlife refuges, and five national forests. Each state also has large tracts of its land controlled by the federal Bureau of Land Management (BLM) (National Wildlife Federation 1990). In addition to these holdings, there are national recreation areas, state parks, state historical monuments, state refuges, and a host of other entities that control or limit use to various parcels of land in the desert states.

Compounding use and access problems to public lands, as described above, are established or pending wilderness designations that put in place another layer of "management" and use limitations, with accompanying allowances and requirements for activities. Innumerable organizations, groups, and societies have, or wish to have, a claim on these "desert lands," and they expect or demand to help determine how the lands are managed and maintained. These groups each have an agenda for the use and care of public lands in the western deserts. These agendas include a wide range of philosophies representing bird-watching groups, hiking societies, river runners, trail users, research groups, livestock interests, boy scouts and girl scouts, Rocky Mountain big horn sheep hunters or protectors, elk hunters, outdoor recreationists, wolf societies, and wildlife conservation groups; the list is almost endless. Most of the groups are very vocal and very well organized.

Use of and demand for access to these lands in the western deserts are not decreasing or leveling off, but are increasing each year. Taking national nonconsumptive wildlife use (those uses exclusive of harvest or taking) as a barometer, the following comparisons are made. The number of Americans sixteen years of age or older participating in nonconsumptive wildlife use changed from 93.2 million in 1980 to 134.7 million in 1985 (United States Department of the Interior and United States Department of Commerce 1982, United States Department of the Interior 1988), an increase of 44.5%. The proportion of these people visiting all public and federal lands also increased dramatically. Indeed, in 1985 fully 16% of the population took trips to observe, photograph, or feed wildlife.

These data reveal an enormous pressure on resources. In the western states the major pressure will be on public resources because they constitute the majority of available lands. Constantly increasing pressure for nonconsumptive use will increasingly require good stewardship, wise planning, and thoughtful and insightful management if we as a nation are to continue to provide the opportunity for outdoor recreation that is so much a part of our national heritage. Conflicting policies between agencies of the federal government, as well as conflicting policies and goals between state and federal land management agencies, are a detriment to the resources and resource values of the desert West. It is essential that all user groups and advocacy groups see their agendas addressed in national planning efforts. Only through common goals can agencies, users, advocates, and protectionists achieve a promising future for these valuable resources. If we can reach this harmony we will ensure the usefulness and existence of the values present in the deserts. If we fail to achieve harmony, irrevocable loss of irreplaceable resources and loss of an unknown amount of biodiversity is certain to occur.

THREATS TO DESERT AQUATIC ECOSYSTEMS: A SUMMATION

Functions and events that threaten either a species or the aquatic ecosystem on which it depends are actually few in number and can be summarized as follows. Species are directly threatened with extinction by predation, diseases, and parasites; competition and/or hybridization (with exotics); and poisonings by pesticides, herbicides, or other chemicals. Species are threatened indirectly by habitat (ecological) change. Ecosystems are threatened by destruction by filling, draining, pumping, dredging, and so on, or alteration by thermal change, water-flow changes, or introduction of non-native plants or organisms.

CONCLUSIONS

Viewing western desert resources and their management without becoming aware of the inherent conflicts associated with that enterprise is difficult. Whether using a desert spring to sustain livestock on a BLM allotment is given higher priority than the activity of those seeking solitude and solace in a far-off wild place, certain resource values must exist to achieve those requirements. The bureaucracy associated with the management of western desert resources is staggering in its size and complexity. Federal offices (in Washington, D.C.), regional offices, and state offices, as well as local-use districts, compounded by state, central, regional, and local offices, produce a myriad of policies, personalities, and goals. A given policy in one district may be unacceptable in an area with similar resources located only miles away and under a different state or federal management unit.

We were tempted to raise the flag, often waved in the last decade, of single-agency administration and management of all western public lands (combined U.S. Department of Agriculture, Forest Service, Department of the Interior, Fish and Wildlife Service, and Bureau of Land Management, at a minimum) as a solution to the bureaucracy, and in fact, we incorporated that concept in an early draft of this manuscript. As one reviewer noted, however, that would be an administrative (read: *bureaucratic*) solution to a biological problem. A uniform policy of natural resource development (some would read: *exploitation*) has been implemented across the western public lands by the myriad federal agencies.

What is needed is not a new agency but, rather, a new *biological* policy. Is this nation, and the West, to protect and enhance wilderness areas and unique aquatic habitats, or let them, and their unique endemic species, follow others into extinction?

This biological policy must be grounded in sound science, coupled with realistic fiscal support, and implemented with sufficient expedience to halt extinctions and habitat degradation in all areas of the arid West. Particular attention must be given to wilderness areas where resource values are most closely tied to the rationale for the wilderness, where resource values are most cherished, and where slight impacts today can have monumental consequences tomorrow.

ACKNOWLEDGMENTS

We gratefully acknowledge review and comment by Margaret B. Sigler, Sydney Peterson, Anne Flannery, Thom Hardy, Ed Marston and Dick Carter, as well as the editors of this volume, Sam Zeveloff and Cy McKell.

REFERENCES

Baugh, T. M., and J. E. Deacon. 1983. "The Most Endangered Pupfish." *Freshwater and Marine Aquarium* 6:22–26, 78–79.

Bender, G. L. 1982. "Introduction." In G. L. Bender (ed.) *Reference Handbook of the Deserts of North America*. Westport, Conn.: Greenwood Press, pp. 1–6.

Constantz, G. D. 1981. "Life History Patterns of Desert Fishes." In R. J. Naiman and D. L. Soltz (eds.) *Fishes in North American Deserts*. New York: John Wiley and Sons, pp. 237–290.

Cross, J. N. 1975. "Ecological distribution of fishes of the Virgin River (Utah, Arizona, Nevada)." M.S. thesis, University of Nevada, Las Vegas.

Deacon, J. E., T. B. Hardy, J. Pollard, W. Taylor, J. Landye, J. Williams, P. Gregor, and M. Conrad. 1980. "Environmental Analysis of Four Aquatic Habitats in East-central Nevada, June-September 1980." Report for Henningson, Durham, and Richardson. Las Vegas, Nevada: Environmental Consultants Incorporated.

Deacon, J. E., and J. E. Williams. 1984. "Annotated List of the Fishes of Nevada." *Proceedings of the Biological Society of Washington* 97:103–118.

Johnson, J. E. 1987. *Protected Fishes of the United States and Canada*. Bethesda, Md.: American Fisheries Society.

Kennedy, C. H. 1916. "A possible enemy of the mosquito." *California Fish and Game* 2:179–182.

LaRivers, I. 1962. *Fishes and Fisheries of Nevada*. Reno: Nevada State Fish and Game Commission.

Miller, R. R. 1943. "*Cyprinodon salinus*, a New Species of Fish from Death Valley, California." *Copeia* 1943:69–78.

———. 1981. "Coevolution of Deserts and Pupfishes (Genus *Cyprinodon*) in the American Southwest." In R. J. Naiman and D. L. Soltz (eds.) *Fishes of the North American Deserts*. New York: John Wiley and Sons, pp. 39–94.

Miller, R. R., and E. P. Pister. 1971. "Management of the Owens Pupfish, *Cyprinodon radiosus*, in Mono County, California." *Transactions of the American Fisheries Society* 100:502–509.

Minckley, W. L. 1973. *Fishes of Arizona*. Phoenix: Arizona Game and Fish Department.

Minckley, W. L., D. A. Hendrickson, and C. E. Bond. 1985. "Geography of Western North American Freshwater Fishes: Description and Relationships to Intracontinental Tectonism." In E. O. Wiley and C. H. Hocutt (eds.) *Zoogeography of North American Freshwater Fishes*. New York: Wiley Interscience, pp. 519-613.

Naiman, R. J. 1981. "An Ecosystem Overview: Desert Fishes and Their Habitat." In R. J. Naiman and D. L. Soltz (eds.) *Fishes of the North American Deserts.* New York: John Wiley and Sons, pp. 493–531.

National Wildlife Federation. 1990. *Conservation Directory.* Washington, D.C.: National Wildlife Federation.

Pflieger, W. L. 1975. *The Fishes of Missouri.* Jefferson City: Missouri Department of Conservation.

Robbins, C. R., R. M. Bailey, C. E. Bond, J. R. Brooker, E. A. Lachner, R. N. Lea, and W. B. Scott. 1980. *A List of Common and Scientific Names of Fishes from the United States and Canada.* 4th ed. Special Publication No. 12. Bethesda, Md.: American Fisheries Society.

Sigler, W. F., W. T. Helm, P. A. Kuchera, S. Vigg, and G. W. Workman. 1983. "Life History of the Lahontan Cutthroat Trout, *Salmo clarki henshawi,* in Pyramid Lake, Nevada." *Great Basin Naturalist* 43:1–29.

Sigler, W. F., and R. R. Miller. 1963. *Fishes of Utah.* Salt Lake City: Utah Department of Fish and Game.

Sigler, W. F., R. R. Miller, and J. W. Sigler. 1992. *Fishes of Utah.* Rev. 2d ed. (In Press)

Sigler, W. F., and J. W. Sigler. 1986. "History of Fish Hatchery Development in the Great Basin States of Utah and Nevada." *Great Basin Naturalist* 46:583–594.

Sigler, W. F. and J. W. Sigler. 1987. *Fishes of the Great Basin.* Reno: University of Nevada Press.

Sigler, W. F., and G. W. Workman. 1978. *The Bonneville Cisco of Bear Lake, Utah–Idaho.* Research Report no. 33. Logan: Utah Agricultural Experiment Station.

United States Department of the Interior and United States Department of Commerce. 1982. *1980 National Survey of Fishing, Hunting, and Wildlife Associated Recreation.* United States Superintendent of Documents. Washington, D.C.: United States Government Printing Office.

United States Department of the Interior. 1988. *1985 National Survey of Fishing, Hunting and Wildlife Associated Recreation.* Washington, D.C.: United States Superintendent of Documents. Washington, D.C.: United States Government Printing Office.

World Book Encyclopedia. 1988. Chicago: World Book Incorporated.

APPENDIX

Common and Scientific Names of Fishes Listed in the Text*

*Following Robbins et al. as revised for the 1990 edition (in review).

Family Cyprinidae
Carps and Minnows

Chiselmouth	*Acrocheilus alutaceus* Agassiz and Pickering
Common Carp	*Cyprinus carpio* Linnaeus
Utah Chub	*Gila atraria* (Girard)
Tui Chub	*Gila bicolor* (Girard)
Humpback Chub	*Gila cypha* Miller
Bonytail	*Gila elegans* Baird and Girard
Roundtail Chub	*Gila robusta* Baird and Girard
Virgin River Spinedace	*Lepidomeda mollispinis mollispinis* Miller and Hubbs
Woundfin	*Plagopterus argentissimus* Cope

Colorado Squawfish	*Ptychocheilus lucius* Girard
Relict Dace	*Relictus solitarius* Hubbs and Miller
Redside Shiner	*Richardsonius balteatus* (Richardson)

Family Catostomidae
Suckers

Utah Sucker	*Catostomus ardens* Jordan and Gilbert
Tahoe Sucker	*Catostomus tahoensis* Gill and Jordan
Cui-ui	*Chasmistes cujus* Cope
June Sucker (extinct)	*Chasmistes liorus liorus* Jordan
June Sucker (present)	*Chasmistes liorus mictus* Miller and Smith
Razorback Sucker	*Xyrauchen texanus* (Abbott)

Family Salmonidae
Trouts and Salmons

Bear Lake Whitefish	*Prosopium abyssicola* (Snyder)
Bonneville Cisco	*Prosopium gemmiferum* (Snyder)
Bonneville Whitefish	*Prosopium spilonotus* (Snyder)
Cutthroat Trout	*Oncorhynchus clarki* (Richardson)
Lahontan Cutthroat Trout	*O. c. henshawi* Gill and Jordan
Bonneville Cutthroat Trout	*O. c. utah* Suckley
Sockeye Salmon (Kokanee)	*Oncorhynchus nerka* (Walbaum)
Brown Trout	*Salmo trutta* Linnaeus
Lake Trout	*Salvelinus namaycush* (Walbaum)
Arctic Grayling	*Thymallus arcticus* (Pallas)

Family Cyprinodontidae
Killifishes

White River Springfish	*Crenichthys baileyi* (Gilbert)
Devils Hole Pupfish	*Cyprinodon diabolis* Wales
Amargosa Pupfish	*Cyprinodon nevadensis* Eigenmann and Eigenmann
Owens Pupfish	*Cyprinodon radiosus* Miller

Salt Creek Pupfish	*Cyprinodon salinus* Miller
Pahrump Killifish	*Empetrichthys latos latos* Miller

Family Poecillidae
Livebearers

Western 　Mosquitofish	*Gambusia speciosa* (Baird and Girard)

Family Centrarchidae
Sunfishes

Striped Bass	*Morone saxatilis* (Walbaum)
Sacramento Perch	*Archoplites interruptus* (Girard)
Bluegill	*Lepomis macrochirus* Rafinesque
Largemouth Bass	*Micropterus salmoides* (Lacepède)
Black Crappie	*Pomoxis nigromaculatus* (Lesueur)

Family Cottidae
Sculpin

Utah Lake Sculpin	*Cottus echinatus* Bailey and Bond
Bear Lake Sculpin	*Cottus extensus* Bailey and Bond

6

LIVESTOCK USE IN ARID LAND WILDERNESS AREAS: CONCERNS OF THE RANCHING INDUSTRY

Cyrus M. McKell, Christopher A. Call,
and G. Allen Rasmussen

INTRODUCTION

Wilderness, legally defined as an area where the earth and its community of life are untrammeled by man and where man himself is a visitor who does not remain (United States Congress 1964), appropriately describes millions of acres of unique and remote lands in arid regions of the western United States. In response to public demand, Congress passed the Wilderness Act of 1964 (United States Congress 1964), which established a process for creating a National Wilderness Preservation System. The Act called for the designation of large expanses (>5,000 acres) of roadless and remote public lands to protect their ecological, geological, historical, and scenic values. The only allowed uses were foot and horse travel, hunting and fishing, backpack camping, nonmotorized boating, scientific study, and continuance of existing mining and grazing uses with no expansion. The Act ignored semiarid and arid public lands administered by the Bureau of Land Management (BLM). With its passage in 1976, the Federal Land Policy and Management Act (FLPMA) (United States Congress 1976) required a study of all BLM roadless areas (>5,000 acres) for wilderness potential. While Wilderness Study Areas (WSAs) are under review, they are to be managed in a manner to preserve their wilderness character, subject to continuation of existing grazing and mining uses. By 1980 the BLM had determined that approximately 150 million acres of the initial 174 million acres of roadless area inventory lacked appropriate wilderness characteristics. By 1986, the BLM had designated twenty-three wilderness areas, totaling approximately 369,000 acres, and was studying nearly 25 million acres in nine hundred roadless areas for their wilderness potential (Coggins and Wilkinson 1987).

Heated controversy surrounding the amount of land to be designated and

93

the policies for their future management testifies to the wide range of opinions that exist on the subject. The most difficult issues appear to be designation of which lands should be set aside, as well as determination of the most important criteria for management of users and their impacts on the land. Among those who claim to speak on wilderness issues, opinions concerning the purpose of and need for wilderness range from the philosophical to the practical. The old adage that "beauty is in the eye of the beholder" could not be more true when listening to the numerous voices describing the virtues of wilderness and the many viewpoints on ways to manage these scenic and remote lands. To some wilderness users, the presence of livestock, mainly cattle and sheep, on WSAs constitutes an unwelcome intrusion. Somehow, the presence of feral horses and burros, or descendants of domestic livestock, does not appear to create the same sense of unwelcome, and wildlife is highly desired. On the other hand, many people enjoy seeing cattle or sheep in wilderness areas as part of the scene that calls up visions of cowboys, Indians, and early western history. Perceptions and experiences, or the lack thereof, of people in positions of authority dominate public land policy formulation, which, in turn, cause misinterpretations of the laws that set national policy. For example, the word *untrammeled,"* used in the definition of *wilderness* in the Wilderness Act, was carefully selected to reflect a condition of being "left to operate freely"; but it has been misinterpreted by federal agency review teams to mean "untrampled" (Crandell 1987). This interpretation may prompt federal land managers to reduce livestock trampling impacts by reducing livestock numbers on WSAs. Thus, people in the livestock industry face increasing difficulty and bureaucratic discouragement in their use of federal rangelands, especially wilderness areas, for livestock grazing.

The anxiety of ranching families about continuing grazing in wilderness areas is not fully calmed by the promise of Congress that uses that exist at the time of wilderness designation would remain a part of the land management agency's operational plan. Even though existing uses may not be arbitrarily terminated, nor regulated solely with a view to preserving wilderness character, they may be regulated in order to prevent unnecessary or undue degradation to the land (Coggins and Wilkinson 1987). In addition, slogans such as those from extremist groups (for example, Earthfirst!) calling for public lands to be "livestock-free by 93" create concern in livestock groups because of the general public's ready acceptance of such slogans and its lack of understanding of natural resource management. Pressure of public opinion on federal land managers and congressional committees could lead to further restrictions on the use of federal lands for livestock grazing.

The situation is further complicated by biased reports depicting the entire ranching industry as being abusive and possessive of rangelands, as well as those that tend to depict all environmental groups as extremist organizations that want public rangelands for their exclusive use. Uncontrolled grazing by cattle and sheep in the late 1800s and early 1900s on arid rangelands, where large herbivores had not previously occurred with regularity, led to land degradation that is still evident today. At that time, livestock producers did not understand the ecology of the forage resource, nor did they have a full appreciation of the erratic precipitation and prolonged dry periods that made these systems so vulnerable to mismanagement. A better understanding of plant and animal needs and improved management practices (proper animal numbers, proper season of grazing, water developments) (McKell and Norton 1981) now make it possible to manage grazing so that rangeland conditions on 87% of BLM lands are stable and improving (United States Department of the Interior 1990).

The livestock industry is important to the economy of most rural communities in the West and depends on public rangelands that have been used traditionally for grazing under the supervision of federal and state rangeland managers. The ranching industry is not as concerned with the process of designating wilderness areas under provisions of the Wilderness Act as it is with administrative restrictions and rules governing access and maintenance of facilities such as water developments, trails, and fences needed to control livestock. Many in the ranching industry fear that wilderness designation will open the way for additional restrictions of livestock use. With few exceptions, livestock allotments on WSAs and adjacent federal lands are an integral part of each ranching operation and rural community. Thus, any management changes on federal lands will impact rural ranching families and communities.

The purpose of this chapter is to provide some examples of the importance of grazing in WSAs to adjacent ranches and rural communities; to review the language Congress used in describing the conditions under which livestock use could continue in areas where it existed prior to designation of wilderness; and to discuss some issues regarding livestock use of public lands that are designated as wilderness.

EXISTING LIVESTOCK USE OF ARID LANDS
PROPOSED FOR WILDERNESS

All western states have some arid and semiarid lands administered under the BLM that sustain livestock use. As an example, in Utah the BLM administers 1,467 grazing allotments for the livestock of 1,815 permittees on twenty-two million acres. Grazing use on BLM lands amounts to 6,003,372 animal unit months (AUMs). This amount of grazing use would accommodate 1,000,562 head of cattle for six winter months in the deserts and lowland ranges of the state. If supplemented by three months of grazing on Forest Service allotments in high mountains and three months of grazing on home ranch property, a total livestock population of approximately one million head of cattle or equivalent animal units (in which one horse equals one animal unit or five sheep equals one animal unit) could be sustained year-round. However, the actual numbers of livestock grazing on BLM lands in Utah in 1983 were 143,139 cattle and 434,120 sheep, considerably less than the number of permits available. Clearly, not all of the permitted AUMs are used each year because of unfavorable weather conditions that influence the production of herbage and successional changes which alter forage availability. Even so, the number of animals permitted to graze on federal lands is critical to the livestock industry and to rural communities. Without supplemental periods of grazing on public lands, the number of animals that could be accommodated on the home ranch would not be economical in most situations.

A substantial loss of permitted AUMs in wilderness grazing would create a serious impact on the western livestock industry. According to the Utah BLM Statewide Wilderness Draft EIS (United States Department of the Interior 1986), a maximum of 423 permittees have grazing permits inside 82 WSAs and hold permits for 96,521 AUMs of grazing use (Table 6.1). Data presented in the EIS indicate that an estimated 1,970,720 dollars are spent in local communities by ranchers to sustain the livestock that graze on WSAs. Using a multiplier of two times the base value for the economic effect of these funds (Snyder and Lewis 1989), the value to the local economies of Utah is approximately 4 million dollars. This is minimal compared to the value added to ranch properties that utilize grazing on federal land and thus augment the productive capacity of the ranch property (Workman 1988).

Grazing permits held by permittees must meet the test of commensurability (Stoddart et al. 1975), which means that a livestock operator must have private lands that are commensurate or "match up" with the federal grazing permit. This arrangement was developed early in the history of American range management to ensure that adjacent rangelands would be used to round out the seasons of grazing use and to create optimal use of both private and public lands. The system also gave priority to local owners of private land rather than to distant livestock owners who might be less consistent in their year-to-year grazing use and less committed to following good management practices because of little or no incentive to properly manage their animals to protect the range for future use. The result of the commensurability requirement is that present-day ranch operators depend heavily on their federal grazing permits to sustain the home ranching enterprise.

Continued livestock use of areas designated as wilderness could be subjected to increased problems resulting from a failure to maintain facilities such as wells, springs, drift fences, and corrals. Many areas have had range improvement projects, and others have been planned. According to the draft EIS (United States Department of the Interior 1986), maintenance of existing facilities and improvement projects would be subject to wilderness standards and EIS procedures designed to optimize wilderness values. Any projects that

Table 6.1.   Grazing Use in Wilderness Study Areas of Utah[1]

Region of State	Number of Allotments	Number of Permittees	Number of AUMS in WSAs	Value of Local Sales
West Central	39	85	25,019	$ 500,385
South West	130	355	26,377	527,160
South Central	35	160	10,534	215,040
East Central	97	196	38,325	550,585
South East	26	58	8,295	167,550
Totals	327	854	108,510	$1,960,720

[1]Source of information: United States Department of the Interior. 1986. Utah BLM Statewide Wilderness Draft Environmental Impact Statement.

required motorized heavy equipment or vehicles to maintain the projects would be seriously reviewed and open for public comment. The net result of this public pressure would undoubtedly result in a reduction in the number of permitted AUMs as well as greater difficulty in managing the livestock on wilderness areas in spite of congressional commitment that livestock uses existing at the time of wilderness designation could continue.

CONGRESSIONAL COMMITMENT TO CONTINUE GRAZING IN WILDERNESS AREAS

In writing the legislation of the Wilderness Act, the intent of Congress was to allow grazing to continue in wilderness areas where its prior use had existed. Undoubtedly, members of Congress recognized the great disruption that would occur to rural communities if grazing were terminated. Implicit in the language of the Act is the intent that grazing would be regulated by the federal agencies according to well-established principles of resource management and public review. The objective of section 4(d)(4)(2) of the Wilderness Act is to:

> Utilize the forage resource in conformity with established wilderness objectives for each area and the BLM grazing regulations and through practical, reasonable and uniform application of the congressional guidelines and policy.

To provide further guidance, the United States Congress (1980) prepared a Conference Report (House Report 96-1126) which clarified its intent for dealing with the main issues related to continuance of grazing in National Forest Wilderness Areas. The language of 96-1126 was intended to cover all grazing management regardless of agency jurisdiction. During the Ninety-fifth Congress, congressional committees became increasingly disturbed that after over fifteen years of developing management policies, national forest administrative regulations and policies were acting to discourage grazing in wilderness or unduly restrict various activities necessary for proper grazing management. Subsequently, two House committees wrote reports (House Committee on Interior and Insular Affairs Reports 95-620 and 95-1321) as to how section 4(d)(4)(2) of the Wilderness Act should be implemented. The five main issues emphasized in these reports should provide assurance to those in the livestock industry who are obliged to depend on BLM managers and policymakers to follow the congressional guidelines in specific management situations:

1. There should be no curtailment of grazing in wilderness areas simply because of wilderness designation, nor should managers "slowly phase out" grazing through overly rigorous operating requirements. Adjustments of AUMs should be made only on the basis of normal grazing and land management planning and policy-setting process.

2. Maintenance of supporting facilities such as fences, wells, cabins, and stock tanks, existing in an area prior to classification as wilderness is permissible and may be accomplished through the occasional use of motorized equipment where practical alternatives do not exist.

3. Replacement or reconstruction of deteriorated facilities in wilderness areas is permissible and need not always be accomplished with "natural materials," given reasonable cost equalities.

4. Construction of new improvements or replacement of deteriorated facilities in wilderness is permissible if done in accordance with guidelines and management plans governing the area. New improvements should be made primarily for the purpose of resource protection and effective management.

5. Use of motorized equipment for emergency purposes is permissible for such problems as livestock rescue or placement of emergency feed. This provision should not be abused by the permittees.

The rule of thumb that Congress mandated federal agencies to follow in carrying out the intent of the enabling legislation is that activities or facilities established prior to the date of wilderness designation should be allowed to remain in place and may be replaced whenever necessary. Further, Congress intended to closely monitor implementation of the guidelines through subsequent oversight hearings and agency annual reports.

MAJOR ISSUES IN CONTINUING GRAZING USE OF DESIGNATED WILDERNESS AREAS

The livestock industry has singled out as the most important concern for the future of grazing use on wilderness areas the need for the BLM and other federal agencies to maintain management practices consistent with the policy of the Wilderness Act and congressional committee guidelines regarding uses and facilities existing at the time of designation.

The usual management planning and implementation activities carried out by BLM personnel, such as writing and revising allotment management plans, rangeland analysis, maintaining structural and nonstructural range improvements, and planning needed new improvements, must be carried out with opportunities for public review. Too often, however, advocates for wilderness and livestock groups with negative feelings for either the legitimacy or the needs of wilderness and grazing users may speak out in public meetings or utilize various media opportunities to press their viewpoints. This polarization has complicated the land manager's ability to plan properly responsible levels of livestock use to maintain the resource.

Another issue of critical importance to ranchers is the solution to the problem of state school sections within wilderness areas. In Utah, up to 330,114 acres of state trust lands are either inheld or adjacent to WSAs (Governor's Advisory Council on Inter-governmental Affairs 1986). These lands are managed by the Board of State Lands and Forestry to create revenues by grazing leases and mineral leases and harvesting forestry products, as appropriate, for the uniform school fund. In the past, grazing use of these state sections has generally followed the management restrictions and policies of the BLM. Should these lands receive increased restrictions in use as a result of wilderness designation, or if necessary motorized access is restricted, the level of educational income could be reduced.

Two concerns are created by this uncertain future: (1) that management criteria may differ in state versus federal areas where there is no clear demarcation between them; and (2) if a permittee were able to enhance the grazing capacity of his allotment on state land through various improvement practices, would he be faced with maintaining a specified number of livestock on one part of his allotment and another number of stock on the balance of the same allotment? The BLM could prevent range manipulations on adjacent federal lands to preclude the possibility of having disparate carrying capacities on the same allotment.

Further, the position of the federal government is not clear regarding the future of the state school trust lands. The EIS states that the BLM does not intend to acquire the state lands. However, the state of Utah has proposed that certain parcels of state-owned lands be exchanged for public lands in other areas (Matheson 1983, 1984; Bangerter 1985).

Interactions between domestic livestock and wildlife on western rangelands have been a matter of concern to resource managers and environmentalists for many years, and they have centered on direct competition for forage resources, changes in vegetation composition caused by livestock grazing, social conflicts, and alteration of wildlife home ranges through water developments and fencing arrangements (Hall 1985). Direct and indirect effects of livestock management on wildlife can be adverse or complimentary depending upon habitat type, the management program, and the species involved. For example, because of social conflicts, bighorn sheep will move to less desirable areas or concentrate on remaining habitat when they encounter livestock (Van Dyke et al. 1983). On the other hand, 98% of all lands occupied by pronghorn antelope are in dual use with domestic livestock, primarily cattle (Yoakum 1980). Cattle, horses, and sheep are more dependent on grasses than pronghorns, which have a high preference for forbs at all seasons (Wagner 1978). Significant competition between livestock and pronghorn antelope would not be anticipated as long as all classes of forage were in adequate supply. Research has shown that carefully managed spring grazing by cattle, sheep, horses, or goats can retain or improve winter habitat for mule deer (Urness 1990). Unfortunately, land managers largely have been unable or unwilling to use livestock to manipulate vegetation composition for the improvement of wildlife habitat on arid and semiarid rangelands.

Continued maintenance of an effective predator-control program is another concern of the livestock industry, if grazing use is to continue in wilderness areas. It may seem logical to the wildlife manager to maintain populations of predator wildlife species in wilderness areas, but not when the number of predators increases to the point that predation causes unbearable economic losses of livestock. Under such conditions, grazing simply may not be able to continue even though the BLM grazing permit is available. In the EIS guidelines for specific activities, predator control is allowed on a case-by-case basis where control is necessary to protect threatened or endangered wildlife species or to prevent special and serious losses of domestic livestock. Obviously, the rancher must have already sustained big losses to justify a predator-control activity. Allowed methods must target the offending individuals and present the least possible hazard to other animals or wilderness visitors.

A clear showing must be made that the removal of the offending predators will not diminish the wilderness values of the area. Lucas (1987) compiled reports of a conference on needed research for wilderness, yet no mention was made of predator problems. Obviously, there is a need to analyze the impact of predator-control policy in wilderness areas. To those in the livestock industry, the current policy for predator-control appears so restrictive that they fear grazing may not be able to continue as an economic use in wilderness areas. A possible alternative to the removal of offending animals is the use of guard dogs to deter predators. Guard dogs have been effectively used by the Navajo to protect flocks of sheep and goats from coyotes in the Southwest (Black and Green 1985). Guard dogs, however, would only be part of an integrated predator-management plan.

From 1946 to 1976, the BLM's only statutory management mandate was the Taylor Grazing Act of 1934 (United States Congress 1934), which contemplated neither multiple-use nor formal land-use planning, except in a primitive fashion (Coggins and Wilkinson 1987). Thus, livestock grazing was the traditional dominant use. The Federal Land Policy and Management Act of 1976 (United States Congress 1976) does not repeal the major Taylor Act provisions, but it does superimpose a new multiple-use management system on BLM lands. An interpretation of FLPMA could support the conclusion that livestock grazing has been downgraded from the major rangeland use to an undifferentiated one of several uses, and that livestock producers are not entitled to priority in resource allocation (Borman and Johnson 1990). Understandably, the livestock industry may now feel that the emphasis in wilderness management has shifted to recreational use and preservation, and is not in the true spirit of multiple-use management. All uses generate at least some conflict with regard to management decisions, and it will be difficult to accommodate those who represent a single use. Coggins (1984) predicted protracted legal delays and litigation before wilderness designation will take place and operate in a workable fashion. Thus, the result will be insecurity for ranchers and wilderness proponents in working with BLM land managers. The ranchers will be concerned with management decisions that will reduce livestock-carrying capacity, while wilderness proponents will be concerned about management decisions that reduce the value of wilderness areas.

Rather than resorting to confrontation and conflict in the courts, we should be attempting to bring diverse interest groups together to communicate their concerns to each other and to form a consensus plan on how to manage wilderness areas and WSAs so that everyone can ultimately benefit (Borman and Johnson 1990). One process that is becoming increasingly important and sophisticated is Coordinated Resource Management Planning (CRMP) (Banner et al. 1989). This planning process involves resource owners, managers, users, and organizations of interested people, allowing them to help in developing the management plan. All goals and decisions must have at their core the maintenance of the integrity of the resource. The CRMP group must have open, direct communication, reach their management decisions by consensus, and follow the management of an area to ensure that the goals they set are being accomplished. If the goals are not being achieved, the management must be changed. The CRMP process has been successful in solving numerous land-use conflicts in the western United States, and it could reduce the use of litigation in determining wilderness land-use policies.

REFERENCES

Bangerter, N. 1985. "Comments on state land preliminary draft narrative." Letter to state BLM office. Office of the Governor, Salt Lake City, Utah.

Banner, R. E., M. A. Barney, C. M. Johnson, R. D. Harrison, and J. C. Jensen. 1989. *Utah Coordinated Resource Management and Planning Handbook and Guidelines*. Extension Circular no. 436. Cooperative Extension Service, Logan: Utah State University.

Black, H. L., and J. S. Green. 1985. "Navajo Use of Mixed-breed Dogs for Management of Predators." *Journal of Range Management* 38:11–15.

Borman, M. M., and D. E. Johnson. 1990. "Evolution of Grazing and Land Tenure Policies on Public Lands." *Rangelands* 12:203–206.

Coggins, G. C. 1984. "Public Rangeland Management Law: FLPMA and PRIA." In *Developing Strategies for Rangeland Management*. A report prepared by a Committee of the National Research Council, National Academy of Sciences. Boulder, Colo.: Westview Press, pp. 1901–1976.

Coggins, G. C., and C. F. Wilkinson. 1987. *Federal Public Land and Resources Law*. 2d ed. Mineola, N.Y.: Foundation Press, Inc.

Crandell, H. 1987. "Congressional Perspectives on the Origin of the Wilderness Act and Its Meaning Today." In R. C. Lucas (comp.) *Proceedings—National Wilderness Research Conference: Issues, State-of-Knowledge, Future Directions*. United States Department of Agriculture Forest Service General Technical Report INT-220, pp. 9–14.

Governor's Advisory Council on Inter-governmental Affairs. 1986. "Consolidated Local Government Response to the Utah BLM Statewide Wilderness Draft Environmental Impact Statement." Office of the Governor, Salt Lake City, Utah.

Hall, F. C. 1985. *Wildlife Habitats in Managed Rangelands—The Great Basin of Southeastern Oregon: Management Practices and Options*. United States Department of Agriculture Forest Service and United States Department of the Interior Bureau of Land Management General Technical Report PNW-189. Portland, Ore.: Pacific Northwest Forest and Range Experiment Station.

Lucas, R. C. (comp.) 1987. *Proceedings—National Wilderness Research Conference: Issues, State-of-knowledge, Future Directions*. United States Department of Agriculture Forest Service General Technical Report INT-220.

Matheson, S. 1983. "Utah State Policy on Wilderness Areas and State Land Exchanges." Letter to state BLM office. Salt Lake City: Utah State Capitol.

———. 1984. "Identification of Utah State Land In-holdings Needing Exchange in Wilderness Areas." Letter to state BLM office. Salt Lake City: Utah State Capitol.

McKell, C. M., and B. E. Norton. 1981. "Management of Arid Land Resources for Domestic Livestock Forage." In D. W. Goodall, R. A. Perry, and K. M. W. Howes (eds.) *Arid Land Ecosystems: Structure, Functioning and Management*. Cambridge, England: Cambridge University Press.

Snyder, D. L., and W. C. Lewis. 1989. *The Size and Role of Agriculture in Utah*. Research Report no. 129. Logan: Utah Agriculture Experiment Station, Utah State University.

Stoddart, L. A., A. D. Smith, and T. W. Box. 1975. *Range Management*. 3d ed. New York: McGraw-Hill.

United States Congress. 1934. Taylor Grazing Act of 1934. Washington, D.C.: United States Government Printing Office.

———. 1964. Public Law 88-577. The Wilderness Act of 1964. 88th Congress. Washington, D.C.: United States Government Printing Office.

———. 1976. Public Law 94-579. The Federal Land Policy and Management Act of 1976. 94th Congress. Washington, D.C.: United States Government Printing Office.

———. 1980. Grazing in National Forest Wilderness Areas. Conference Report on S.2009, House Report 96-1126. Washington, D.C.: United States Government Printing Office.

United States Department of Interior. 1986. *Utah BLM Statewide Wilderness Draft Environmental Impact Statement*. Utah BLM Office, Bureau of Land Management. 6 vol. Washington, D.C.: United States Government Printing Office.

———. 1990. "State of the Public Rangelands 1990: The Range of Our Vision." (brochure). Washington, D.C.: Bureau of Land Management.

Urness, P. J. 1990. "Livestock as Manipulators of Mule Deer Winter Habitats in Northern Utah."

Paper presented at Symposium—Can Livestock Be Used as a Tool to Enhance Wildlife Habitat? 43d Annual Meeting of the Society for Range Management, Reno, Nevada.

Van Dyke, W. A., A. Sands, J. Yoakum, A. Polenz, and J. Blaisdell. 1983. *Wildlife Habitats in Managed Rangelands—The Great Basin of Southeastern Oregon: Bighorn Sheep.* United States Department of Agriculture Forest Service General Technical Report PNW-159. Portland, Ore.: Pacific Northwest Forest and Range Experiment Station.

Wagner, F. H. 1978. "Livestock Grazing and the Livestock Industry." In H. P. Brokaw (ed.) *Wildlife and America.* Washington, D.C.: United States Government Printing Office, pp. 121–145.

Workman, J. 1988. "Federal Grazing Fees: A Controversy That Won't Go Away." *Rangelands* 10:128–130.

Yoakum, J. 1980. *Habitat management guides for the American pronghorn antelope.* United States Department of the Interior Technical Note 347. Denver: Denver Service Center.

7

DEFENDING THE DESERT

Dick Carter

In Utah, the debate over BLM wilderness triggers an inordinate amount of emotion. Not only is there conflict among classic opponents (environmentalists and development interests), but conflict waged between northern and southern Utahans as well as rural and urban residents. Federal land-management agencies exhibit strenuous conflicts over management of the canyon country or the much larger Great Basin. Although both the Bureau of Land Management, the predominant federal land manager in the West, and the National Park Service are within the Department of the Interior, their perceived missions, and consequently actual management, differ dramatically. Border disputes are not uncommon. Add to the fray the U.S. Forest Service, often the "headwaters" manager, and a half-dozen state agencies guided by much more narrow principles, and it is not at all uncommon to see acrimonious battles between state and federal agencies. With the howling of environmental organizations and local governmental entities, it is common to encounter land-management dilemmas.

Now you've got to wonder why. Let's go back about two hundred million years. The canyon country was on the west coast of the supercontinent Pangea. Rather than a plateau, it was most similar to the present Sahara Desert, consisting of a massive lowland desert of sand. As Pangea began to split up over tens of millions of years in a remarkably disrupting process, the canyon country was either a submerged ocean accumulating oceanic sediments or a vast arid region accumulating inland sediments from the high ground of what is now North America. About ten million years ago, western North America was uplifted, which increased precipitation and provided for the beginning of a massive erosional process of splitting these sediments into the present-day Colorado River system.

The result was an unmatched physical landform. That is one reason this place creates so much conflict—it is unique. It has been carved by wind and rain, lifted, dropped, and scorched, and has resulting in canyons and cliffs, bridges and arches, fins, buttes, and mesas stained in red, yellow, buff, and purple that all change with the rising, setting, and seasonal angle of the sun.

It is a physical attraction mirrored nowhere except possibly in a few bizarre dreams delivered by our subconscious.

It is massive. The Great Basin, largely composed of western Utah and almost all of Nevada, is the size of France. The Colorado Plateau of southern Utah, western Colorado, northern Arizona, and northwestern New Mexico encompasses some 130,000 square miles. In Utah alone, the BLM has identified some 3.2 million acres of Wilderness Study Areas (WSA) with environmentalists proposing anywhere from four to five million acres. Thus, literally, the last wilderness debate will take place on lands as unique as any on the globe.

This remarkable physical expression of the Colorado Plateau has been acknowledged through numerous national parks, monuments, recreation areas, scattered wildernesses, and a number of state parks. Utah's nine national parks, monuments, and recreation areas divulge not only a stunning geological story but preserve some of the most rugged terrain in North America. Other noteworthy parks, monuments, and recreation areas consist of the Grand Canyon, Mesa Verde, Canyon de Chelly, Dinosaur, Hovenweep, and over twenty congressionally designated wildernesses, numerous historical sites, and designated natural landmarks.

The Great Basin has received less attention, but with the recent passage of the Nevada Wilderness Act the area now harbors over a dozen wildernesses along with Great Basin National Park, which straddles the high country of the Snake River Range dominated by Wheeler Peak.

And, of course, the uniqueness of these arid lands, whether in the Great Basin or the Colorado Plateau, has prompted the Bureau of Land Management Wilderness Review and calls for the expansion of many of the national parks in the region as well as the creation of new parks such as a proposed San Rafael National Park in east-central Utah.

In 1985, and again in 1986, the state of Utah submitted a lengthy proposal for a Colorado Plateau Thematic World Heritage List nomination to the U.S. Department of the Interior, further indicating both the uniqueness of the region and the growing attention being given to arid lands for biological, recreational, and aesthetic values.

In the process of telling this geological story of arid lands on the Colorado Plateau, for example, we have preserved it in something other than a textbook. These areas have become reservoirs of endangered species, clean air, wild and free-flowing rivers, and unmatched aesthetics. Our fondness for these unique values has led Zion and Bryce national parks in Utah to consider a public transportation system to eliminate congestion similar to the crowds of Yosemite and Old Faithful. River trips through the famed whitewater of Westwater Canyon, Desolation Canyon, the Grand Canyon, and the Yampa have been controlled for years now by a controversial permit system. The irony of waiting for a permit to get on a wild river has escaped nobody. And permits are needed for backpacking trips in places like the Grand Gulch Primitive Area (proposed wilderness) or the Paria Canyon Wilderness, not because of some sort of land-management power play, but because there are so many users in such a confined and fragile environment.

But with a bit of good-natured schizophrenia, environmentalists have for years rallied behind the idea that these arid lands were the hidden treasure of undiscovered wilderness. Sitting high on the green slopes above the desert, environmentalists seemed to be wondering what is down there.

They are anything but hidden. The same geologic story harbored in the exposed redrock canyon country which has produced this unmatched landscape has also produced uranium-bearing rocks, extensive low sulfur-producing coal seams, large oil and gas fields, and open space. Open space not just for aesthetic contemplation, if you will, but for the roar of off-road vehicles. There is something powerful, apparently, to be gained by roaring unconstrained beneath the buttes and above the canyons. There are more straight lines to pursue than forested environments. There are fewer bogs than subalpine parklands. Dust and emptiness.

And then there are cows. When, in the mid-1800s, the first white settlers arrived (Mormon leader Brigham Young dispatched these parties from the Salt Lake Valley, a veritable oasis compared to the places to which they were sent to in western and southern Utah), it was obvious the rain shadow and high evaporation rates of the exposed interior were going to prevent a broad-based cultivation-type agricultural society. There loomed that open space again—turn the cows out and let them search for a blade or two of grass.

Those dark crusty peds on the surface of the soil were probably not understood by early Mormon pioneers. The rambunctious lot of present-day motorized, two- and three-wheelers doesn't appear to notice them or to care. Range managers have no excuses, but until recently they have shown little interest in these cryptogamic crusts. Literally as pockets on the slickrock and scattered throughout the canyon country, these spore-producing communities of algae, lichens, or mosses hold the barren soils together, produce a bit of organic matter, and create a marginally favorable microclimate, making succession to flowering plants a possibility. It is well known that these soils are as fragile as any, particularly sensitive to the tire or hoof.

Water is at the center of every debate simply because it is so rare. Ironically, water defines these arid lands, from the biological potential of riparian areas to the indefatigable geological beauty. And the aridity combined with almost no urban development creates vistas unmatched in North America. Clear air is the norm. Nonetheless, these conflicts in resource allocation are not textbook conflicts; they are real and they add immense pressure to any resolution.

SCRUBBY FORESTS . . . OR WILDERNESS?

So are these arid lands wilderness or wasteland? The majority of the Great Basin or the Colorado Plateau simply does not meet the definition of *wilderness* provided in the Wilderness Act of 1964. Although most of the land base is administered by BLM (only federal lands can be designated as *wilderness* under the Wilderness Act), it is exceedingly obvious that the rest of the definition of *wilderness* dramatically restricts the size of the potential wilderness resource in our arid western public lands:

> A wilderness in contrast with those areas where man and his own works dominate the landscape, is hereby recognized as an area where the earth and its community of life are untrampled by man, where man himself is a visitor who does not remain. An area of wilderness is further defined to mean in this Act, an area of undeveloped Federal land retaining its primeval character and influence, without permanent improvements or human habitation, which is protected and managed so as to preserve its natural conditions and which (1) generally appears to have been affected primarily by the forces of nature, with the imprint of man's work substantially unnoticeable; (2) has outstanding opportunities for solitude or primitive and unconfined type of recreation; (3) has at least five thousand acres of land or is of sufficient size as to make practicable its preservation and use in an unimpaired condition; and (4) may also contain ecological, geological, or other features of scientific, educational, scenic, or historical value.

It is well-known history that to get the Wilderness Act through Congress in the early 1960s, after eight years of contentious debate, grazing was allowed to continue where and how it was established on an area prior to designation. Without this caveat it is very clear that few, if any, arid lands would qualify as wilderness. But the founders of the National Wilderness Preservation System realized after this lengthy debate that wilderness could not be held to a standard unrepresentative of our tremendous impact upon this continent. Wilderness, to go solely beyond an idea, had to forego that puristic wish. But even in 1964 Congress had no idea of what the arid public domain harbored. Those public lands were still managed by a host of desert land entry acts dating back to our earliest frontier years and the Taylor Grazing Act of the early 1930s.

How could there be wilderness? No lakes, or mountains. Only scrubby forests and rangelands managed for cows. Culturally, our focus on wilderness had been those high, snow-covered sawtooth peaks. The debate centered on that terrain, further emphasizing the fact that arid lands weren't worthy of the debate. Our image of wilderness was not that of a native southwestern American; rather it was the image, both real and romantic, of a native European.

It wasn't until 1976, with the passage of the Federal Land Policy and Management Act (FLPMA), that this image was ameliorated. Congress had been convinced that the BLM needed (1) a formal "organic" act, (2) a consistent planning process, and (3) an opportunity to identify lands that may qualify as wilderness.

This wilderness review was initiated in the late 1970s and utilized a multistep process of a "quick" initial inventory to delete lands clearly and obviously lacking wilderness values. The second step was an intensive inventory to define wilderness study areas. This step was nothing but a more detailed initial inventory using the very specific criteria in the Wilderness Act: naturalness, outstanding opportunities for solitude and primitive and unconfined recreation, and other special values. It was not until the third step, an actual study, that Congress instructed the BLM to weight these WSAs against other land uses, or "manageability" as wilderness, and determine whether these WSAs would be "suitable" or "unsuitable" for wilderness recommendation.

The FLPMA required the president to make a final recommendation to Congress by 1991. The process has been a lengthy one, filled with public input. While it places a high degree of credibility on the BLM's recommendations, Congress realized that wilderness designation is responsive to public concerns and that agencies such as the BLM have powerful land-management biases. Nationwide, the BLM has identified about twenty-four million acres of WSAs. In Utah, this, like most wilderness issues, has been a contentious debacle.

In a challenge led by the Utah Wilderness Association, the 1980 Intensive Inventory was appealed to the BLM's adjudication board, the Interior Board of Land Appeals. The IBLA agreed with the environmental objections, remanding over 825,000 acres of the 900,000 + acres appealed back to the BLM for further study. The BLM simply refused to acknowledge that wilderness characteristics were present. This and one subsequent appeal filed by the same groups resulted in the BLM increasing the acreage of WSAs from the 1980 proposal of 2.6 million acres to the final decision of 3.2 million acres. In 1986, Utah's BLM office acknowledged that about 1.9 million acres of the 3.2 million acres should be recommended to the president as suitable, with the rest being unsuitable because of resource tradeoffs. This figure was bumped up almost 100,000 acres with the final recommendation in 1990.

Not even Utah environmental groups see eye to eye on the BLM, a fact hardly surprising, given the very essence of this land. But their recommendations are much larger than BLM's, ranging from four to five million acres. And not surprisingly, Utah's politicians have staked out not-so-new territory, with Congressman Owens supporting the largest of the environmental community's proposal of 5.1 million acres. Congressman Hansen has supported 1.4 million acres. Utah's county commissioners have formally opted for "zero."

Well over a decade has passed and the nation has concluded that, indeed, arid lands belong in the wilderness system. Clearly, many arid western BLM lands meet the definition of *wilderness*. They represent some of the most unique and environmentally constrained lands in North America. And our cultural and societal appreciation of wilderness is growing. Wilderness is not simply a recreational resource, but is now perceived as an opportunity to maintain biotic diversity and to meet a host of spiritual and cultural values placed at the top of our domestic agenda. Yet very few BLM areas have been designated, even though Arizona, Utah, and California are presently pursuing wilderness designation.

Whether the hanging gardens, consisting of individually unique plant associations at each seep or spring emerging from water-saturated sandstone formations, alcoves, "waterpockets," buttes, pinnacles, or the two dozen or so major mesas, the Colorado Plateau represents an exhilarating biological and aesthetic resource.

Ironically, it is the canyons that define the Colorado Plateau in the same manner as dozens of mountain ranges define the Great Basin. The names of these canyons say more than words can describe: Grand, Desolation, Marble, Cataract, Labyrinth, Westwater, Dark, Happy, Woodenshoe, Parunuweap, Zion, Buckskin, Paria, Dirty Devil, the Virgin . . . and hundreds of others.

This canyon system, linked together by the tributaries of the Colorado River, likely represents the single largest network of canyons in any recognized geological province on earth. Desolation and Grand canyons are over a mile deep and provide an unmatched sense of space. Paria Canyon, a few hundred feet deep and only a few feet wide in places, restricts the view of the sky above for one backpacking at times through waist-deep water.

Add to the canyons the natural bridges, mesas, hogsback ridges, the seventy-mile-long San Rafael Reef, broad desolate valleys, pinnacles, towers, mesas, buttes, arches, desert bighorn sheep, mountain lions, a half-dozen rare or endangered fish species, whitewater as wild as any place on the planet in Westwater, Desolation, Cataract or the Grand Canyon, and the idea of wasteland disappears quickly as an arrogant human domination of a landscape. Wilderness? Yes. Wasteland? Only where we have removed the intrinsic and native character of this landscape.

A REGIONAL APPROACH TO BLM WILDERNESS IN UTAH

In Utah, for example, the BLM and environmentalists have identified roughly nine geographically linked wilderness regions. While the acreage proposed for wilderness differs dramatically, the wilderness character in each region is sufficiently different that a brief description is warranted to portray the remarkable panoply of Utah's arid wildlands.

The West Desert

The Great Basin vastness of Utah's west desert, for example, is punctuated by a series of mountain ranges that rise steeply and tower over the wide valleys. The high country provides ecological diversity, serving as habitat for raptors, mountain lions, and bighorns. The mountains are also an irreplaceable source of water that once sustained Pony Express riders and wagon trains, and that today is used by nearby ranches.

The magnificent Deep Creek Mountains are every bit as spectacular as the Great Basin National Park in Nevada. Ibapah Peak rises eight thousand feet from its base on the Great Salt Lake Desert to summits twelve thousand feet above sea level. The high alpine country is drained by perennial streams that harbor relic cutthroat trout. Rare stands of bristlecone pine and ancient cave pictographs can be found.

Notch Peak in the House Range is a sheer limestone monolith of over three thousand feet, rivaling those in the Sierra Nevada. The surrounding mountains are noted for their impressive fossil beds and stands of aspen and fir. Golden eagles are common, and the endangered peregrine falcon finds habitat in the region.

Zion/Cannan Mountain

The beauty of southwestern Utah is characterized by Zion National Park, but this corner of Utah is actually a transition zone for three major bioregions—the Great Basin, the Mojave/Sonoran, and the Colorado Plateau. Joshua trees, Gila monsters, and the endangered desert tortoise are found nowhere else in Utah. The Zion/Cannan Mountain proposal reflects such diversity.

Yet the scenic heart of this area lies in the spectacular redrock canyons of the Virgin River and the adjacent wild country. Parunuweap Canyon, whose name means "roaring waters," is divided between Zion National Park and BLM land. The canyon is over seven hundred feet deep and only twenty feet wide at the narrows. First explored by John Wesley Powell just over one hundred years ago, it remains as he found it—remote, cathedrallike, and subject to wild flash floods as the East Fork of the Virgin River carves ever deeper into the sandstone.

Cannan Mountain borders Zion on the south. It is a high plateau, forested with ponderosa pine and sheer redrock slopes. Habitat for bighorn sheep and mountain lions is found in this remarkably wild and colorful region.

Desolation/Book Cliffs

Desolation Canyon of the Green River has often been compared to the Grand Canyon in scale—from the plateaus to the river it is over a mile deep.

The Book Cliffs are one of the world's longest and most spectacular escarpments. Together, they form one contiguous wilderness proposal of 600,000 acres of BLM land.

The whitewater trip through the rapids of Desolation and Gray canyons has long been one of the most popular in the West. This stretch of the river has been declared a national historic landmark in commemoration of the Powell expeditions, and it is inhabited by three endangered species of fish. Fremont petroglyphs are found in profusion. Side canyons such as Rock Creek and Range Creek could be wilderness areas in their own right, with an amazing diversity in vegetation and wildlife. High above the river, the Tavaputs Plateau harbors Rocky Mountain bighorn sheep.

Remote and looking deceptively barren in their lower elevations, the Book Cliffs and Roan Cliffs rise to nine thousand feet. On top, they are forested with ponderosa pine, aspen, and Douglas fir. This is some of the most highly valued year-round wildlife habitat in Utah, with elk and black bear thriving in the high, rugged country.

San Rafael

The San Rafael region is like a composite of all of Utah's national parks. Indeed, it has long been under consideration as an addition to the national park system, with the Utah Wilderness Association formally proposing approximately 300,000 acres as a national park. The region harbors massive sandstone monoliths; narrow, winding river corridors; uplifted reefs; arches; slot canyons; and knobs.

Saddle Horse Canyon, the Little Grand Canyon, the Wedge, and Chimney Rock enliven the area. Mexican Mountain harbors the towering Window Blind Peak and the Black Box, a literal chasm carved by the San Rafael River. It is also crucial desert bighorn sheep habitat and provides a haven for about a dozen rare and endangered plant species.

Kaiparowits Plateau

The Kaiparowits is a tremendous expanse of wild country stretching from the Paria River on the west to the Straight Cliffs, fifty miles east. Remote canyon systems, sweeping vistas, and significant archeological and paleontological resources characterize the area.

Paria-Hackberry is a huge complex of canyons below the headwaters of the Paria River southeast of Bryce Canyon National Park. Bull Valley Gorge and Deer Creek Canyon are two of the best-known canyons. Numerous unnamed natural arches, colorful badlands, and views of the Cockscomb, White Cliffs, and Vermillion Cliffs add scenic interest. The top of No Man's Mesa has scientific value for its relic plant associations.

Fifty Mile Mountain, adjacent to National Park Service–proposed wilderness in Glen Canyon National Recreation Area, is a vast mesa bordered by the Straight Cliffs on one side and cut by dozens of canyons on the other. BLM has identified over three hundred archeological sites, including rock art and ancient cliff granaries; 37,800 acres are proposed for protection under the National Historic Preservation Act.

Other areas include Wahweap, with sheer-walled canyons, hoodoos, balanced rocks, and fourteen-hundred-year-old juniper trees along with Carcass Canyon and its significant fossil beds.

The Escalante

The last-discovered river in the contiguous United States, the Escalante, remains hidden in its unspoiled redrock canyons, but it has become renowned for outstanding wilderness values. The network of tributary canyons is filled with massive arches and alcoves, waterfalls, prehistoric rock art, and deposits of petrified wood. Most BLM units are part of the same roadless areas as the Park Service wilderness proposal in adjacent Glen Canyon National Recreation Area. The entire Escalante would make a wilderness over a half-million acres!

North Escalante Canyons–The Gulch ties together several natural areas previously designated by BLM as outstanding. Harris Wash is a canyon deep enough to impress, but not so large as to overwhelm, a quality shared by the main Escalante.

Phipps–Death Hollow is a continuation of the existing Box-Death Hollow Wilderness in the Dixie National Forest. Phipps is known for the upper and lower Calf Creek Falls and five natural bridges and arches.

Dirty Devil/Canyonlands

This region is centered on Canyonlands National Park and spreads out along the canyons of the Colorado, Green, and Dirty Devil rivers.

In Westwater Canyon, the Colorado thunders through Precambrian "black rock" similar to the Grand Canyon's inner gorge. Although the powerful rapids draw river runners from all over the nation, the side canyons of the area remain little explored. Westwater is also the home of Utah's only nesting bald eagles.

Dark Canyon, a BLM primitive area since 1970, is a complex of three major canyon systems adjacent to the Dark Canyon Wilderness. The canyon walls tower as high as fourteen hundred feet, but the resident desert bighorn sheep bound up the talus slopes with ease. Fable Valley, in the upper reaches of Gypsum Canyon, holds spectacular cliff dwellings left by the Anasazi.

The Dirty Devil includes over one hundred miles of canyons and the Robber's Roost country, once a hideout for Butch Cassidy's Hole-in-the-Wall Gang.

The river can be floated in canoes or kayaks in high water. Prehistoric rock art, deposits of petrified wood, and a beaver colony in Beaver Wash exemplify the diversity of the area.

Grand Gulch

The BLM's Grand Gulch Primitive Area forms the heart of this region, which is a series of canyons that flow into the San Juan River and contain southeastern Utah's largest concentration of Anasazi cliff dwellings and rock art. The entire region is an outdoor museum of Anasazi culture from Whirlwind Draw on the west to Johns Canyon on the east, over two hundred miles of canyons in all. High on ledges, under alcoves, and far up in the heads of side canyons can be found the legacy of a once-proud civilization. Despite looting and vandalism, many sites remain almost the way the ancient ones left them seven hundred years ago. Some have been restored by archeologists.

The Cedar Mesa Complex is a series of canyons that feed into Comb Wash, including lower Mule Canyon, Fish Creek, Owl Creek, and Road Canyon, plus Lime Creek, which enters the San Juan directly. The Cedar Mesa sandstone creates arches, like distinctive Nevills Arch, and erodes into pinnacles and balanced rocks. Cliff dwellings and mesa-top sites need to be conserved for future archeological research.

A few years back I was hiking in a side canyon of the Dirty Devil River, Beaver Canyon. The daytime temperatures in mid-May were already reaching into the mid-90s. I had heard an absurd story of a colony of beaver in this small canyon. The canyon was hot and the water was almost as warm, shallow and muddy. Grazing was minimal, and thus there was a nice riparian habitat. Well, I found those beaver surviving in an environment with extreme constraints. Any disruption of this small creek—any grazing, road building, or mining—and this unique colony was gone. There were no drainages to migrate to, and there are few desert rivers that still approximate both natural flows and natural riparian systems. Our obligation goes far beyond our own spiritual revival because of the unique geology of the area.

WILDERNESS: A CHANCE TO SUCCEED

Wilderness harbors an immense amount of symbolism and imagery. It is an icon. Very few enter the debate without powerful images and perceptions. The dilemma is obvious—because of this symbolism, wilderness is ponderable and that alone contributes to its value and the difficulty in resolving the issue.

While wilderness has probably done more to define our land ethic and our personal, humane, and spiritual values toward land and its life than any other resource, it is clear that wilderness alone will not solve environmental problems facing public lands. We must also focus on ecosystem management across the board as well as extensive restoration and rehabilitation efforts. But wilderness does provide important value-oriented opportunities. It provides an environmental benchmark and has engaged serious ecological investigations into the planet's health. It is a barometer.

But for wilderness to achieve this full potential, the conflicts must be resolved without the protracted and bloody battles unfortunately so consistent with much of the twenty-five-year history of the Wilderness Act.

What is so difficult about seeking consensus or so attractive about a no-holds barred flight? For example, the present BLM wilderness fight here in Utah will do little or nothing to educate and to alter the fundamental problems surrounding resources—that of always looking at natural resources as something to be consumed. Both sides seek to coerce rather than understand. Neither side appears to have an interest in setting in motion the personal and cultural changes that must occur if wilderness is to have any value.

So long as wilderness—in this case, the BLM Wilderness Review—is pursued as the final statement on environmental quality, we guarantee islands of wilderness surrounded by masses of development. Wilderness is one very important issue, but not the only one. For example, too often we conveniently forget that after wilderness is designated, wildlife is still threatened and watersheds are still impacted by too many cattle, sheep, or off-road vehicles. That is because some of the most important habitats and ecosystems do not even qualify as wilderness. Yet they deserve our attention as much as any redrock canyon or high mountain. Wilderness is a piece of the biodiversity puzzle.

If we are to achieve fundamental change in our collective view of the land, we must recognize that it is not a matter of "us versus them." It should be obvious by now that coercing others to alter their value system does not work. There is nothing magical here in Utah, for example, about Congressman Owen's 5.1 million-acre BLM wilderness bill or Congressman Hansen's bill of 1.4 million acres. The need is for pursuit of the real issues. The Utah Wilderness Association has suggested that Owens and Hansen drop their bills and pursue the interests and values inherent to the issue. This, of course, doesn't diminish the vision or purpose of either perspective.

Lofty talk about common ground seems meaningless when opponents of wilderness continue to denigrate it. Their absurd denial must end. It lacks substance from every direction. And believing that environmentalists can or should "roll" their opponents to grab a bigger chunk of wilderness today simply creates losers and seems to denigrate all of the rhetoric about diversity and tolerance from which the environmental movement came. If we cannot pursue this consensus effort, which is far from a passive "let Congress decide for us," and solve wilderness issues with some degree of consensus, success, respect, and dignity, how will we ever address global environmental crises? Wilderness offers us a chance to succeed.

SUGGESTED READINGS

Barnes, F. A. 1986. *Utah Canyon Country*. Salt Lake City: Utah Geographic Series.
Dunne, J. 1989. "Crytpogamic Soil Crusts in Arid Ecosystems." *Rangelands* 11(4):180–182.
Frome, M. 1974. *Battle for the Wilderness*. New York: Praeger Publishers.
Nash, R. 1982. *Wilderness and the American Mind*. New Haven, Conn.: Yale University Press.
State of Utah. 1986. *The Colorado Plateau, a Proposed Thematic World Heritage List Nomination*. Salt Lake City, Utah.
Stegner, W. 1942. *Mormon Country*. Lincoln: University of Nebraska Press.
———. 1987. *The American West as Living Space*. Ann Arbor: University of Michigan Press.
Utah Wilderness Association. 1985. *Defend the Desert, Wilderness Proposals for Utah's BLM Lands*. Salt Lake City, Utah.
Utah Wilderness Coalition. no date. *Utah Wilderness. The Canyon and Desert Lands, How Much to Protect?* Salt Lake City, Utah.

8

ALLOCATING LANDS NOBODY WANTED BUT EVERYONE IS FIGHTING OVER: AN ECONOMIC PERSPECTIVE ON THE OPTIMUM USE OF ARID LANDS

Richard M. Alston

INTRODUCTION

Much has been written about the uniqueness of arid environments and desert landscapes (Woodin 1964). Many resource managers and others have suggested that the uniqueness of semiarid and desert regions calls for an equally unique approach to their use and management (Webb 1931, Malin 1947, Smythe 1969, see also any issue of the *Journal of Arid Lands*; critiques of this approach are found in Smith 1950, Kelso 1967). The idea goes beyond the obvious point that geological, soil, climatic, and even social conditions may vary across tropical, arid, and temperate areas. It is a specific application of the view that "one cannot solve the problems of India by using knowledge and technologies developed for the conditions in Indiana" (Dubos 1971, p. 39).

On one hand are those who seek to develop and exploit arid land resources. This group often suggests that land, particularly desert land, left undeveloped or otherwise not used for commercial purposes is worthless wasteland (Ely and Wehrwein 1940, Barlowe 1972). John Wesley Powell, who led a two-decade-long campaign for the development of the arid region in the nineteenth century, argued that we should do away with the familiar square-grid surveys in the arid region because without stream-side frontage, land was worthless. Powell's main complaint against the rectangular survey was that it produced the survey of unnecessary land. He argued, first, that rectangular land patterns should be discontinued in favor of farms as irregular in shape as was necessary in order to give each parcel frontage on a stream, and, then, that water should be tied to the land (Powell 1962; Alston 1978, pp. 65–71).

If the land is worthless, then no harm, costs, or other negative economic consequences emerge from its use for such things as toxic waste dumps, open pit mining, and military bombing ranges. Others that seek to develop desert resources feel that water is so precious in an arid environment that to bring it onto unused land is good, per se, without reference to a relationship between costs and returns. This viewpoint is implicit in the once-popular phrases "Make the desert blossom as the rose" and "Make two blades of grass grow where but one grew before" (Hirshleifer et al. 1960, Alston 1978).

This group wants society at large to spend hundreds of millions of dollars on the central Utah and central Arizona water projects, which subsidize irrigation agriculture in the desert, while farmers in other parts of the country are going bankrupt. Another current proposal suggests spending twenty million dollars to create a hydroelectric dam on Utah's Fremont River. The proposed development would only provide enough irrigation water to put a mere twelve thousand acres of desert land into production and would produce high-cost electric power (Associated Press 1989). While it is true that such reclamation projects may make the desert bloom, most economists who have studied similar proposals have come to the conclusion that there is little economic justification for the blossoms, particularly when the nation is paying farmers to limit cropland and output (Anderson 1983, p. 52).

A similar issue arose when Congress passed the Taylor Grazing Act in 1934. It gave the secretary of the interior broad discretion to manage the grazing of privately owned livestock on public lands. Grazing fees were set substantially lower than comparable fees on private land because it was felt that to charge the higher price would leave the public range unused and therefore worthless (Dana and Fairfax 1980, Culhane 1981). Of course, the law could have continued the practice of allowing livestock owners free grazing on public land, thereby increasing use even more. The grazing fee, therefore, may be viewed as part of a legislative package aimed at establishing a control strategy that would, nevertheless, favor the interests of the ranchers.

On the other hand, the view that the desert is different is made explicit by those who are inspired by a desire to preserve rather than develop. Environmental groups consistently have sought the imposition of higher fees in order to reduce stocking, thus implicitly arguing that the land is more valuable when used for other purposes such as recreation and wildlife habitat (Wille 1985, Johnson and Watts 1989). (The fact that these users of the public domain do not pay for their uses of the land is taken up later.) Preservationists discount the findings of economic analyses that suggest the most valuable use of desert land is for a nuclear waste dump, massive coal-burning power generators, mineral exploration and mining, livestock grazing, or other commercial developments. Those who hold this view claim that utilitarian economic analysis is not appropriate for desert resource values. They argue that the values of desert species and landscapes are so unique that they ought not be made to pass stringent market tests of relative value (Leopold 1966).

From an economic perspective, however, there is little reason to believe that arid land resources ought to be treated differently than any others. Economics is about choosing among alternatives. The economist asks whether the relationship between social benefits and social costs justifies the development of now commercially idle acres, whether we can afford the blossoms, and whether the extra blade of grass, extra pound of red meat, or nuclear waste dump is worth the cost. It asks, as well, whether foregoing the benefits of commercial development is offset by the gain in wilderness values.

This chapter proceeds as follows. The second section provides a very brief overview of arid land management in the U.S. The third section of the chapter explores how traditional cost-benefit analysis is applied to wilderness decision-making. It describes a new wilderness economics that builds into utilitarian economic accounting the special considerations surrounding the debate on wilderness preservation versus development. The fourth section describes why current institutions that fail to include pricing mechanisms for resource allocation may encourage overdevelopment of land suitable for wilderness classification. It discusses why pricing of environmental amenities may enhance the probability for preservation and the protection of values when wilderness designation is not chosen. The fifth section then turns the arguments in the previous two sections on their heads and suggests why sole reliance on utilitarian cost-benefit criteria may not serve the public interest after all. The sixth section of the chapter concludes by arguing that the process of wilderness designation is a social and political, not an ecological or economic, one. The choice turns on broadly social values, the implementation of which can be aided, but ought not be dictated, by utilitarian economic analysis.

A BRIEF OVERVIEW OF ARID LAND MANAGEMENT

In 1936 the administration of the nonforested arid lands of the West was given over to the Bureau of Land Management (BLM). Following an initial period of acquisition under its ancestral agencies in the nineteenth century, the management objective was to dispose of the land to private owners as quickly as possible. The hope was that commercial development would ensue and the land would be used to grow irrigated crops and graze livestock with subsidized water. Vast areas of arable land were transferred to the private sector, but there were few takers of desert land save for those who entered short-term leases in order to secure mineral resources. After almost one hundred years of custodial management of these "lands nobody wanted," another approach seemed warranted. Following World War II, the BLM entered a period of intensive management. That, in turn, led to what Clawson (1983) calls the period of consultation and confrontation. By 1970 the tracts of desert land and public domain that were unsuitable for private ownership (hence, the "lands nobody wanted") had taken on substantial value to environmentalists and recreationists. It also took on special significance as a potential dumping ground for the country's rapidly accumulating industrial waste and toxic by-products. Battle lines were thus drawn between those interested in developing or exploiting desert land resources and those interested in preserving them.

The earlier view that the land was worthless implicitly accepted a totally static view of history and economic change. But as economic conditions and technology changed, what was previously thought to be worthless wasteland came to have substantial economic (utilitarian) as well as social (nonutilitarian) value. The disposal of the public domain led to a "modern miracle of loaves and fishes"—the more federal land that was given away, the more valuable became that which was left (Clawson 1951, pp. 86–89; Clawson 1983, p. 190). We can be certain that the 1990s will witness an increase in the number of interest groups and individuals fighting for a piece of the action.

The New Wilderness Economics

In response to the above situation, resource planning and analytical models evolved that took into account the newly discovered conflicts and tradeoffs. Utilitarian values were priced and evaluated alongside more traditional commodity outputs. Nonutilitarian values were entered into the models as constraints or (in a very few cases) as new objective functions (Iverson and Alston 1986).

It is beyond the scope and purpose of this chapter to provide a survey of environmental economics (Fisher and Peterson 1976) and cost-benefit analysis (Mishan 1976). But it is appropriate to discuss the emergence of some new economic concepts as they have been applied specifically in the context of wilderness preservation.

Conventional cost-benefit analysis as a decision-making tool for public land management decisions was originally mandated in a provision contained in the Flood Control Act of 1936. The methodology of cost-benefit analysis was originally promulgated in response to that act; it was contained in the Water Resource Council Guidelines. These guidelines, subsequently updated, called for analysis of federal water-related projects in accordance with standards and principles used to evaluate the monetary benefits and costs of each project. Costs and benefits were to be measured on the basis of contribution to national economic development. Cost-benefit analysis also attempted to fully integrate externalities (that is, nonmarket benefits and costs) into the project analysis (Krutilla 1981). The guiding criterion was to be a comparison of benefits and costs measured at market prices or proxies, properly discounted to the present, and counted on the basis of to whom they accrued. The latter provision was interpreted to mean that distributional questions (that is, for whom the resources would be managed, both present and future) were to be considered on the basis that each person was to be treated equally. That is, the willingness to pay for the amenity would be the measure of values obtained and foregone without any special weight given to one individual or group, in the present or the future.

This provision guaranteed adherence to the atomistic and individualistic ideology embedded in orthodox (neoclassical) economic theory. The public interest was thereby defined as the sum of costs and benefits assigned to individuals (although which individual was irrelevant). The whole of the public interest was held to be nothing more or less than the sum of individual utilities. Atomistic individualism, rather than a synergistic holism, became enshrined (Alston 1983). Within the context of that individualistic model, substantial effort went into the development of proxy values that could be used for those outcomes that were not priced in markets (Brown and Goldstein 1984, Brookshire and Coursey 1987, Hoehn and Randall 1987, Neill 1988, Harris et al. 1989).

The traditional cost-benefit approach had asked a rather simple question about the desirability of a project that introduced development into a de facto wilderness: does the flow of benefits of the development project outweigh the flow of costs, both discounted at an appropriate interest rate that made future values commensurate with present values? If the present value of the net benefits were positive, then it was argued that the project passed the test of economic justification. An interesting application of the benefit-cost approach is the siting of nuclear waste dumps and other noxious facilities.

In locating noxious facilities, such as a hazardous waste disposal incinerator, the host community only sometimes garners the direct job benefits while it frequently incurs all of the costs. Meanwhile, other communities in the region or nation receive the diffuse benefits (Kunreuther et al. 1987, p. 371). Why not let individual communities bid on how much they would be willing to pay not to have the facility or, what amounts to the same thing, how much they would have to be compensated in order to accept the facility? Each community would be provided complete information about construction costs, employment benefits, boom-town implications, and so on. Those communities that did not obtain the facility would then finance the project by paying off the recipient community in accordance with the recipient's low bid, which was based presumably on a detailed cost-benefit analysis. In such an auction-bidding game, desert communities with few market-oriented economic opportunities would be the likely recipients. The locals, as has been shown over and over in the case of Utah siting proposals, have a strong affinity for accepting any economic development that comes along. But the utilitarian value of desert wilderness to outsiders would not be captured in such a bidding game. Nor would the nonutilitarian values of the preservation alternative.

Implicit in early cost-benefit analyses was the notion that the preservation option for desert wilderness had neither benefit nor cost. This reflected the long-held view that undeveloped land is worthless. Thus, early cost-benefit analyses did not take into account the likelihood that the values of resource development would decline over time whereas the benefits of preservation would increase over time. It also ignored the fact that not all wilderness values are consumed on site. Moreover, the standard approach did not easily recognize other nonutilitarian values of wilderness preservation.

By the early 1970s, however, a new approach had been developed under the intellectual leadership of Anthony Fisher, John Krutilla, and others at Resources for the Future (Fisher et al. 1972, Krutilla and Fisher 1975). It has since become the conventional economic approach to wilderness preservation (Porter 1982). The new approach rested upon the base of cost-benefit analysis, but added two important dimensions: preservation values and the asymmetry of timing of net benefit flows.

First, the developments in a wilderness area irreversibly destroy any benefits society might have derived from the continued existence of the area in an undeveloped state. These benefits include both those enjoyed by individuals who directly use the wilderness and benefits enjoyed by those who indirectly gain through existence and option values. In the new wilderness, economics would be included in the calculation of both utilitarian benefits and costs.

Existence value is a term applied to the value people place on simply knowing that a park, wildlife refuge, or scenic attraction is being preserved, even though they have no intention of ever visiting the attraction. We may call this the "National Geographic" effect. The economic content of the idea is that people are willing to pay simply for the existence of a natural environment rather than the direct use of environmental amenities.

The concept of option value was first introduced by Weisbrod (1964). Option values represent the value individuals place on preserving an option to visit the natural environment in the future or to preserve it for future generations. The value of preserving options is intimately tied up with the economists' view that present-value calculations may preclude certain persons from participating in the decision. (Page 1977, chapter 7, offers a particularly insightful treatment of the present-value criterion.) Option values also recognize concerns for insufficient knowledge about the synergistic relationships in ecosystems. It is difficult, for example, to identify which threatened or endangered species might prove to be a source of valuable genetic materials. This question, originally raised by environmentalists, represents a utilitarian approach to the preservation of species and explains why economic models of cost-benefit analysis were designed to take them into account.

Moreover, in situations of uncertainty concerning either the benefits associated with development or those of preservation, there may be value in postponing irreversible development. This concept of quasi-option values applied to the value of information was originally introduced by Arrow and Fisher (1974); it was designed to ensure that decision makers did not undertake irreversible development projects if, by postponing action, the information about the future consequences of development would arrive independent of the development itself (Fisher and Hanemann 1987, Hanemann 1989). Clearly, the impact of the development option will be known and uncertainty reduced if the development is undertaken. But reducing the uncertainty may also become available through further research and additional information from similar development projects undertaken elsewhere in the future. Such information would alter the degree of uncertainty and, therefore, the calculation of benefits and costs. This information clearly has utilitarian value. Once the value of future information (hence, quasi-option value) that would become available while maintaining wilderness preservation was built into the analysis, the economic justifiability of a development project could be substantially reduced.

Once preservation values were added to the cost-benefit criterion, any proposed development project faced a new hurdle. Not only did it have to yield net positive benefits, but the overall benefits had to outweigh the discounted flow of net preservation benefits. With the introduction of quasi-option values, these preservation benefits would now include the benefits of reducing uncertainty by waiting for more information.

The second dimension of the new approach was somewhat more innovative. Economists have long argued that the benefits of any particular resource-exploitation activity are likely to ultimately diminish as new technology introduces alternatives to any given development project. Moreover, as the resource is slowly exhausted, extraction and exploitation costs begin to rise. That is, the net benefits decline at some rate over time. On the other side of the coin, however, economists argue that as development continues apace, the benefits of preservation will increase. This asymmetry in the flow of net benefits is largely due to the relatively fixed supply of potential preservation sites and the expected increase in demand for their associated benefits as the population grows and becomes wealthier. The outcome is an exponential rate of decline for development net benefits and an exponential rate of growth of preservation benefits. Hence, the range of the development projects that could be justified according to the cost-benefit criterion became substantially narrowed.

The implications of this new approach were startling to potential desert land and resource developers and preservationists alike. Environmentalists traditionally had opposed the use of a discounting procedure to arrive at present value. When it was used, they argued in favor of using very low discount rates. Why? Because discounting meant that the benefits of preservation that come only in the distant future are trivialized in comparison with present development benefits when high discount rates are used. But the environmentalist abhorrence to the use of discounting was somewhat ameliorated by the new approach. Explicit introduction of the values of wilderness preservation and the quasi-option value of information meant that development projects could fail both because the discount rate was too high and because it was too low. A high discount rate reduced the present value of development benefits while leaving the present value of information available from postponing the development project very high. The new approach, in other words, brought the substantial benefits of preservation forward in time where discounting had less chance to reduce their present value. Preservationists, therefore, could agree with the principle of discounting, turning their attention to why the rate should be low (as opposed to zero).

The second implication was that any project that was deemed to be socially desirable according to the cost-benefit criterion should be expedited. Any delay in its implementation would reduce its ability to pass muster. This, in turn, implied that the preservationist tactic of delaying project initiation through litigation, the courts, and appeals of agency-planning documents was a rational response to achieving their objectives. Indeed, such tactics, while not immediately serving the public interest (as defined in the neoclassical economic model), might prove to have done so in subsequent analysis.

The third implication was somewhat more philosophical. Given the introduction of a decay rate on the benefits of a development project, every consumption-oriented project, independent of its social profitability in the present, would eventually fail to pass muster. The problem, however, is that many investment (as opposed to consumption) projects that yield their benefits far into the future would be deemed desirable, even though it may create burdens on currently poor generations to the benefit of future rich ones. This latter assumption of continued growth in material welfare remains a feature of cost-benefit models in spite of the no- or slow-growth advocates both in and out of the discipline. Daly (1977, p. 99), for example, distinguished between "growthmania"—not counting the costs of growth—and "hypergrowthmania" —counting real costs as benefits. Intergenerational equity remains an unresolved issue since only the current generation can make a decision to develop or preserve. And in economic analysis, the current generation will discount both the benefits and costs passed on to future generations. By discounting the benefits that accrue to future generations from the preservation option, investments in development that yield benefits in the near future are emphasized. Similarly, by discounting the costs that accrue to future generations from the development option, the probability of passing the cost-benefit criterion is enhanced.

USING PRICES TO ACHIEVE OPTIMAL PRESERVATION

It is one thing to argue that decision makers should take account of the existence, option, and quasi-option values of natural environments when determining which lands should be developed and which should be preserved as wilderness. It is another thing to get decision makers to act upon the results of such analysis. Pricing in a model does not provide the same incentives as pricing in a market. Many authors point out that perverse incentives lead land managers to avoid the preservation option, in large part because there have been few ways to increase the agency budget and/or returns to the treasury (Stroup and Baden 1983, O'Toole 1987). This has led some writers to call for privatization of public lands in order to generate revenue as well as to improve efficiency of management by putting resources into the hands of people who must respond to the incentives of the market (Baden 1983).

Economists have good reason to believe that one of the major impediments to efficient management of the public lands and to appropriate levels of wilderness preservation is that many of the resources are not priced and thus do not generate an economic rent. People who use (or hope to use) the resources pay no (or very low) user fees (Anas 1988). This is particularly true for arid and desert lands. Few, if any, user fees are attached to the use of national parks, desert wilderness trails, sand-dune recreational vehicle sites, or wild river experiences. The absence of appropriate fees to cover the cost of management, maintenance, and rehabilitation leads to overuse—not only from an environmental perspective but from an economic one as well.

Economists have built a strong case that the interests of environmentalists would be best served if stiff visitation charges and taxes were imposed to finance the management of desired lands as wilderness areas. Until such prices are established, they argue, wilderness and related natural resources will be treated as if they possess no value. This argument is properly extended to explain why congestion and degradation of natural environments can be expected to decrease the amenity benefits and overall quality of natural environments, even after they have been placed in the wilderness preservation system.

One may reject the economic criterion of cost-benefit analysis to determine which lands will be zoned for preservation by creating national parks, wilderness areas, and wildlife refuges. But it must be recognized that such designation often attracts more visits, increases congestion, and often causes more environmental degradation than the absence of the zoning. Anas (1988) shows that pricing of wilderness resources prior to final allocation will improve environmental quality and, if used properly, will result in more land preservation. Appropriate pricing policies include visitation charges and recreation quotas. Including severely high taxes to be used for mitigation in the analysis of development projects may also reduce the tendency for development options to be favored over preservation options. Pricing, in other words, may or may not establish the basis for wilderness zoning. But whatever decisions are made in that regard, pricing via appropriate fees and quotas can serve to enhance and protect the desired environmental values in both designated and undesignated wilderness areas.

WHY ECONOMIC ANALYSIS IS NOT ENOUGH

Economists feel that wilderness uses ought to be priced in the marketplace or an equivalent proxy developed. These resource uses include recreation, water, grazing rights, mineral claims, wildlife, scenic vistas, and other elements of the wilderness experience. A great deal of time and energy has been expended by economists to ensure that cost-benefit analysis gets the prices right. Why? Because prices matter! Distorted prices (that is, those that don't reflect actual market transactions) or zero prices (outcomes that are treated as free goods) get weighed right along with all the others. Getting the price right is critical, therefore, to economic analysis. The problem is that while there are practical reasons to accept market prices and their analytical proxies as correct, there is no theoretical reason to do so. Prices found in the real world reflect distortions from the theoretically pure market model that lays behind cost-benefit analysis. They are not the prices of pure theory. Thus, even if analysts could find market prices and mimic them when using analytical proxies for untraded goods, no matter how perfectly done it would not get at the central issue of wilderness preservation.

At issue is the fact that we are dealing with competing ideologies. Economics is designed to assess the means by which utilitarian objectives (taken as given) are achieved. Environmentalism, on the other hand, is aimed at questioning the acceptability of utilitarian policy objectives—the ends (Maxwell and Randall 1989).

Market prices are used to measure benefits and costs to whomsoever they accrue. But other than vague attempts to distinguish between the good and bad by counting them as benefits and costs, the market cannot discriminate between what many consider to be the morally good and bad. The market, for example, cannot distinguish between the actions of people willing to pay a fortune to go to the desert to drive their four-wheel drive vehicles up and down the hillsides and sand dunes, on the one hand, and the gentle footsteps of a bird watcher, on the other. Indeed, the former, according to the market, is worth more than the latter (the vehicle being worth more than the pair of binoculars).

The real issue is not what people are willing to pay to use the public domain and desert land, but which uses will be permitted and what the user fees will be (Alston 1988). The problem with the neoclassical approach to cost-benefit analysis is that it has no mechanism to measure social and collective values apart from individual values as expressed in the market. As Irland (1979) put it:

> The debate over wilderness preservation is a debate over values; it cannot be resolved in a market setting. The values are conflicting orientations towards nature. One orientation sees nature in instrumental [utilitarian] terms—as a source of commodities, hiking opportunities, or research projects. The other orientation sees nature as intrinsically valuable, as contributing to wider and more durable human purposes than do aluminum billets or carloads of coal. Because the stakes are so high, the nation's preservation policies become a contest over whose values are to prevail—those of industry, those of preservationists, or those of the resource management agencies.

Mark Sagoff (1988) argues that the neoclassical economic principles of efficiency, welfare maximization, and cost-benefit balancing arbitrarily confuse the social definition of goals with the satisfaction of individual desires. He and others (Alston 1983) argue that environmental ethics require that individual desires be tempered with collective values and socially determined goals. Social and environmental regulation should be guided by what we stand for "as nation, not simply what we wish to buy as individuals" (Sagoff 1988, pp. 16-17). Sagoff emphasizes that economic analysis is critical to the determination of what is feasible. We may want a perfectly clean environment, but resources to accomplish that goal are simply beyond our reach. Thus, he argues, "economic analysis has much to contribute not only in discovering the least costly methods to accomplish social goals but also in determining what these goals should be" (Sagoff 1988, pp. 216–217). In this context, the Wilderness Act, the Endangered Species Act, the National Environmental Policy Act, the National Forest Management Act, and the Federal Land Policy and Management Act are viewed not simply as mandates for economically efficient management, but as mandates to pursue the social and ethical goals contained in them.

Thus, ethical, political, economic, and social information are critical to informed decision making. The issues are complex and the heartfelt pleas to consider nonutilitarian values are no replacement for rigorous models that are a "prerequisite to having anything convincing to say to either group" (Maxwell and Randall 1989, p. 247). Economic models used to organize and analyze complex information are our best tools for testing various assumptions and hypotheses, particularly those involving tradeoffs and choices among alternatives. They may be of less use in sorting through the ideological debates about which paradigms and which values should guide social decision making.

CONCLUSION

This chapter has been directed primarily at the economic criterion for judging alternative uses of desert land (that is, as wilderness or commercially developed wasteland). The conclusion reached here is that goals and objectives of land classification and zoning for preservation ultimately must be based upon social and ethical principles. This choice must be made in a manner that reflects a collective interest that goes beyond the market summation of individual interests. The market and price system can be captured in economic models that become valuable tools in the socially optimal allocation of resources. They are considerably less useful as means to identify and choose among alternative goals and to establish legitimacy of alternatives. Economics takes tastes, preferences, and values as given—it has no basis for weighing one person's wants against another's, no criteria beyond utilitarian and individualistic values for judging legitimacy among goals. Its philosophical justification for pursuing this use of desert land over that use is atomistic when many call for a holistic approach to the problem.

Economists are correct in asserting that individuals, bureaucrats, land managers, and citizens remain the ultimate source of policy decisions concerning which lands will be zoned for wilderness preservation and which shall be fully or partially developed for resource exploitation. But those individuals are relied upon for informed judgment about society's interest. Let there be no question. Those individuals will pursue their own self-interest in response to the incentives they face. The challenge is to create incentives that guide self-interested bureaucrats to make the public interest their own. Society's interest, neoclassical economic assumptions notwithstanding, goes beyond the summation of the willingness of individuals to pay, adjustments for market externalities, and utilitarian estimates of willingness to pay for existence, option, and quasi-option values. Society's growing interest in wilderness resource management reflects the fact that market failure, externalities, and irreversibilities are pervasive.

REFERENCES

Alston, R. M. 1978. *Commercial Irrigation Enterprise, the Fear of Water Monopoly, and the Genesis of Market Distortion in the Nineteenth Century American West*. New York: Arno Press.

———. 1983. *The Individual vs. the Public Interest: Political Ideology and National Forest Policy*. Boulder, Colo.: Westview Press.

———. 1988. "Reforming the Forest Service: a Review." *Ecology Law Quarterly* 15:503–517.

Anas, A. 1988. "Optimal Preservation and Pricing of Natural Public Lands in General Equilibrium." *Journal of Environmental Economics and Management* 15:158–172.

Anderson, T. 1983. *Water Crisis: Ending the Policy Drought*. Baltimore, Md.: Johns Hopkins University Press.

Arrow, K. J., and A. C. Fisher. 1974. "Environmental Preservation, Uncertainty, and Irreversibility." *Quarterly Journal of Economics* 88:312–319.

Associated Press. 1990. "Battle Lines Forming Over Fremont Dam Proposal." *Standard Examiner*, Ogden, Utah. 18 February 1990:F1.

Baden, J. 1983. "Privatizing Wilderness Lands: The Political Economy of Harmony and Good Will." P. N. Truluck (ed.) *Private Rights and Public Lands*. Washington, D.C.: Heritage Foundation. pp. 53–70.

Barlowe, R. 1972. *Land Resource Economics: The Economics of Real Property*, 2d ed. Englewood Cliffs, N.J.: Prentice-Hall.

Brookshire, D. S., and D. L. Coursey. 1987. "Measuring the Value of a Public Good: An Empirical Comparison of Elicitation Procedures." *American Economic Review* 77:554–566.

Brown, G., Jr., and J. H. Goldstein. 1984. "A Model for Valuing Endangered Species." *Journal of Environmental Economics and Management* 11:303–309.

Clawson, M. 1951. *Uncle Sam's Acres*. New York: Dodd, Mead Company.

———. 1983. *The Federal Lands Revisited*. Washington, D.C.: Resources for the Future.

Culhane, P. J. 1981. *Public Lands Politics*. Baltimore, Md.: Johns Hopkins University Press.

Daly, H. E. 1977. *Steady-state Economics: The Economics of Biophysical Equilibrium and Moral Growth*. San Francisco: W. H. Freeman and Company.

Dana, S. T., and S. K. Fairfax. 1980. *Forest and Range Policy: Its Development in the United States*. New York: McGraw-Hill.

Dubos, R. 1971. "The Human Landscape." pp. 28–41. In F. Carvell and M. Tadlock (eds.) *It's Not Too Late*. Beverly Hills, Calif.: Glencoe Press. (Originally published in *Bulletin of the Atomic Scientists*, March, 1970, pp. 31–37.)

Ely, R. T., and G. S. Wehrwein. 1940. *Land Economics*. New York: Macmillan.

Fisher, A. C., J. V. Krutilla, and C. J. Cicchetti. 1972. "The Economics of Environmental Preservation: A Theoretical and Empirical Analysis." *American Economic Review* 62:605–619.

Fisher, A. C., and W. M. Hanemann. 1987. "Quasi-option Value: Some Misconceptions Dispelled." *Journal of Environmental Economics and Management* 14:183–190.

Fisher, A. C., and F. M. Peterson. 1976. "The Environment in Economics: A Survey." *Journal of Economic Literature* 14:1–33.

Hanemann, W. M. 1989. "Information and the Concept of Option Value." *Journal of Environmental Economics and Management* 16:23–37.

Harris, C. C., B. L. Driver, and W. J. McLaughlin. 1989. "Improving the Contingent Valuation Method: A Psychological Perspective." *Journal of Environmental Economics and Management* 17:213–229.

Hirshleifer, J., J. C. DeHaven, and J. W. Milliman. 1960. *Water Supply: Economics, Technology, Policy*. Chicago: University of Chicago Press.

Hoehn, J. P., and A. Randall. 1987. "A Satisfactory Benefit Cost Indicator from Contingent Valuation." *Journal of Environmental Economics and Management* 14:226–247.

Irland, L. C. 1979. *Wilderness Economics and Policy*. Lexington, Mass.: Lexington Books, D.C. Heath and Company.

Iverson, D. C., and R. M. Alston. 1986. *The Genesis of FORPLAN: A Historical and Analytical Review of Forest Service Planning Models*. United States Department of Agriculture Forest Service General Technical Report INT-214.

Johnson, R. N., and M. J. Watts. "Contractual Stipulations, Resource Use, and Interest Groups: Implications from Federal Grazing Contracts." *Journal of Environmental Economics and Management* 16:87–96.

Kelso, M. M. 1967. "The Water-is-different Syndrome, or What Is Wrong with the Water Industry." In M. N. Francisco (ed.) Proceedings of the Third Annual Conference of the American Water Resources Association, held in San Francisco, November, 1967. Urbana, Ill.: American Water Resources Association, pp. 76–83.

Krutilla, J. V. 1981. "Reflections of an Applied Welfare Economist." *Journal of Environmental Economics and Management* 8:1–10.

Krutilla, J. V., and A. C. Fisher. 1975. *The Economics of Natural Environments: Studies in the Valuation of Commodity and Amenity Resources.* Baltimore, Md.: Johns Hopkins University Press.

Kunreuther, H., P. Kleindorfer, P. J. Knez, and R. Yaksick. 1987. "A Compensation Mechanism for Siting Noxious Facilities: Theory and Experimental Design." *Journal of Environmental Economics and Management* 14:371–383.

Leopold, A. 1966. *A Sand County Almanac and Sketches Here and There.* New York: Oxford University Press.

Malin, J. C. 1947. *The Grassland of North America, Prolegomena to Its History.* Privately published, Lawrence, Kansas.

Maxwell, J. A., and A. Randall. 1989. "Ecological Economic Modeling in a Pluralistic, Participatory Society." *Ecological Economics* 1:233–249.

Mishan, E. J. 1976. *Cost-benefit Analysis.* New York: Praeger.

Neill, J. R. "Another Theorem on Using Market Demands to Determine Willingness to Pay for Non-traded Goods." *Journal of Environmental Economics and Management* 15:224–232.

O'Toole, R. 1987. *Reforming the Forest Service.* Covelo, Calif.: Island Press.

Page, T. 1977. *Conservation and Economic Efficiency: An Approach to Materials Policy.* Baltimore, Md.: Johns Hopkins University Press.

Porter, R. C. 1982. "The New Approach to Wilderness Preservation through Benefit-cost Analysis." *Journal of Environmental Economics and Management* 9:59–80.

Portney, P. R. 1982. *Current Issues in Natural Resource Policy.* Washington, D.C.: Resources for the Future.

Powell, J. W. 1962. *Report on the Lands of the Arid Region of the United States—with a More Detailed Account of the Lands of Utah.* Wallace Stegner (ed.) Cambridge, Mass.: Belknap Press of Harvard University Press. (Originally published as House Executive Document no. 73, 45th Congress 2d Session, serial no. 1805, 1 April 1878.)

Sagoff, M. 1988. *The Economy of the Earth: Philosophy, Law, and the Environment.* Cambridge, England: Cambridge University Press.

Smith, H. N. 1950. *Virgin Land: The American West as Symbol and Myth.* Cambridge, Mass.: Harvard University Press.

Smythe, W. E. 1969. *The Conquest of Arid America.* Seattle: University of Washington Press, (originally published 1899).

Stroup, R. L., and J. A. Baden. 1983. *Natural Resources: Bureaucratic Myths and Environmental Management.* San Francisco, Calif.: Pacific Institute for Public Policy Research.

Webb, W. P. 1931. *The Great Plains.* New York: Grosset and Dunlap.

Weisbrod, B. A. 1964. "Collective-consumption Services of Individualized-consumption Goods." *Quarterly Journal of Economics* 78:471–477.

Wille, C. 1985. "Cattle Making Desert of West." *Audubon Action* 3:3.

Woodin, A. 1964. *Home Is the Desert.* New York: Macmillan.

INDEX

ABOUT THE BOOK

Wilderness Issues in the Arid Lands of the Western United States
Edited by Samuel I. Zeveloff and Cyrus M. McKell

America is running out of new lands that can be set aside as wilderness. Publically held drylands and deserts in the American West are a large portion of what remains, and the seven essays in this volume address issues involved in designating these arid lands as wilderness. The basic question raised is whether this nation, and the West, will protect and enhance wilderness areas and unique aquatic habitats, or let them and their rare and endangered species of plants and animals follow others into possible extinction.

Too often, dry environments have been seen as areas of limited value. This volume proceeds from the opposite assumption; the chapters show that these drylands are ecologically unique areas worth an extra margin of protection. The management of arid wilderness areas must take into account biological policy—to preserve fragile biotic resources—as well as public policy—to balance economic and political interests of ranching, mining, and recreation with those of environmental protection.

Samuel I. Zeveloff is chair of the Department of Zoology at Weber State University. Cyrus M. McKell is Dean of the College of Science at Weber State University.

CONTRIBUTORS

Richard M. Alston
Department of Economics
Weber State University
Ogden, Utah

Mark S. Boyce
Department of Zoology and Physiology
University of Wyoming, National
  Park Service Research Center
Laramie, Wyoming

Christopher A. Call
Range Science Department
Utah State University
Logan, Utah

Dick Carter
Utah Wilderness Association
455 East 400 South, No. 306
Salt Lake City, Utah

Carl D. Marti
Department of Zoology
Weber State University
Ogden, Utah

Cyrus M. McKell
College of Science
Weber State University
Ogden, Utah

Lee Metzgar
Department of Biology
University of Montana
Missoula, Montana

Wayne Owens
Congress of the United States
House of Representatives
Washington, D.C.

J. Terry Peters
Bighorn Canyon National Recreation Area
P.O. Box 487
Lovell, Wyoming

G. Allen Rasmussen
Range Science Department
Utah State University
Logan, Utah

John W. Sigler
Spectrum Sciences and Software, Inc.
Research and Technology Park
1780 Research Park Way, Suite 106
Logan, Utah

William F. Sigler
Spectrum Sciences and Software, Inc.
Research and Technology Park
1780 Research Park Way, Suite 106
Logan, Utah

Samuel I. Zeveloff
Department of Zoology
Weber State University
Ogden, Utah